COLOR SOCIETY

Spirit Animals Mandalas and More Coloring Book

contents

3 The Tiger
4 The Bull
5 The Unicorn
6 The Cat
7 The Octopus
8 The Wolf
9 The Tortoise
10 The Dragonfly
11 The Dear
12 The Eagle
13 The Dog
14 The Fish
15 The Panther
16 The Jelly Fish
17 The Pig
18 The Owl
19 The Elephant
20 The Ram
21 The Hippopotamus
22 The Horse
23 The Monkey
24 The Frog
25 The Lion
26 The Dolphin

27 The Dragon
28 The Snake
29 The Crab
30 The Fox
31 The Beetle
32 The Bear
33 The Goat
34 The Rabbit
35 The Butterfly
36 The Peacock
37 The Humming Bird

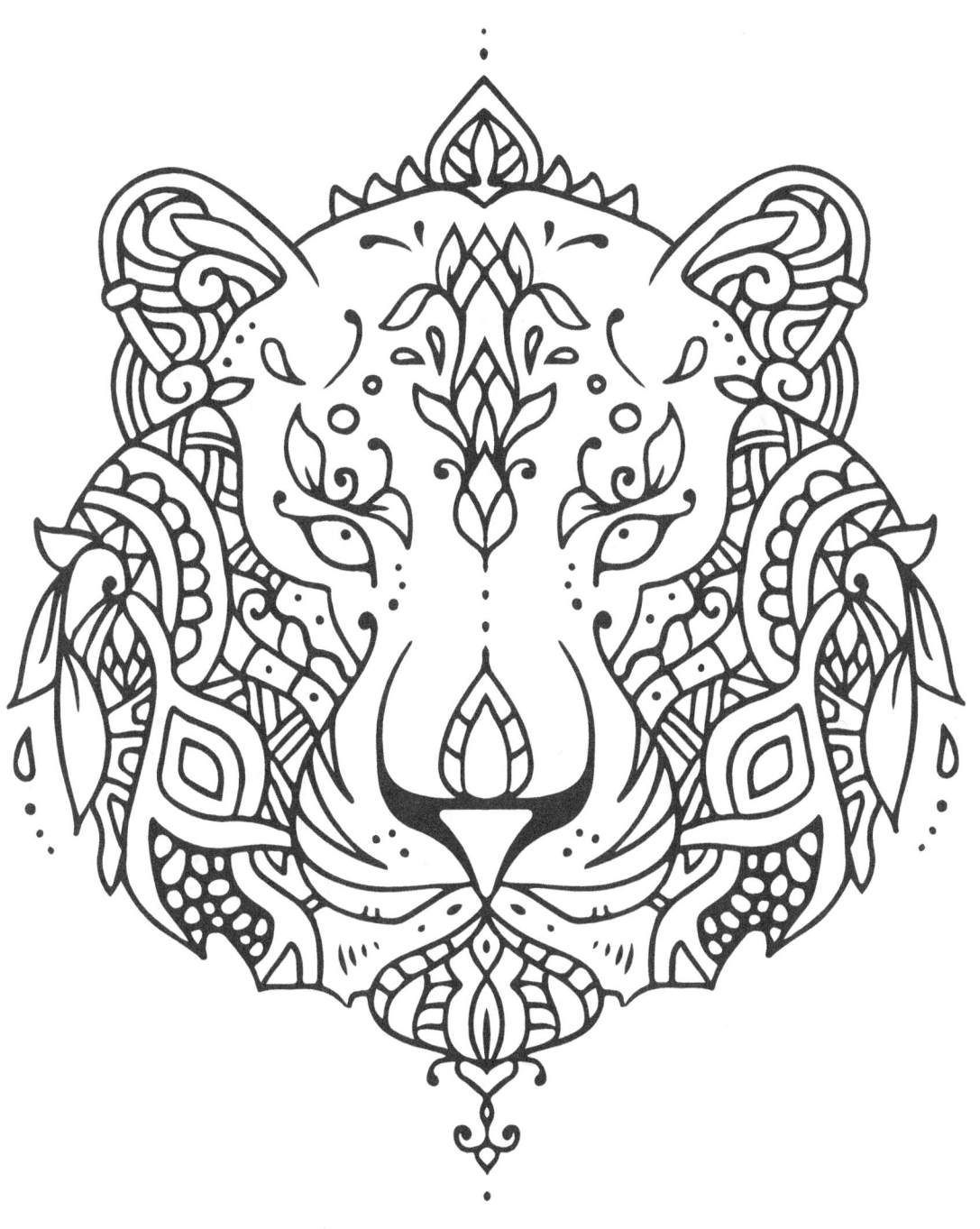

Known as a symbol of confidence and majesty the Tiger signifies vitality and mental energy. The Tiger also symbolizes perseverance and courage.

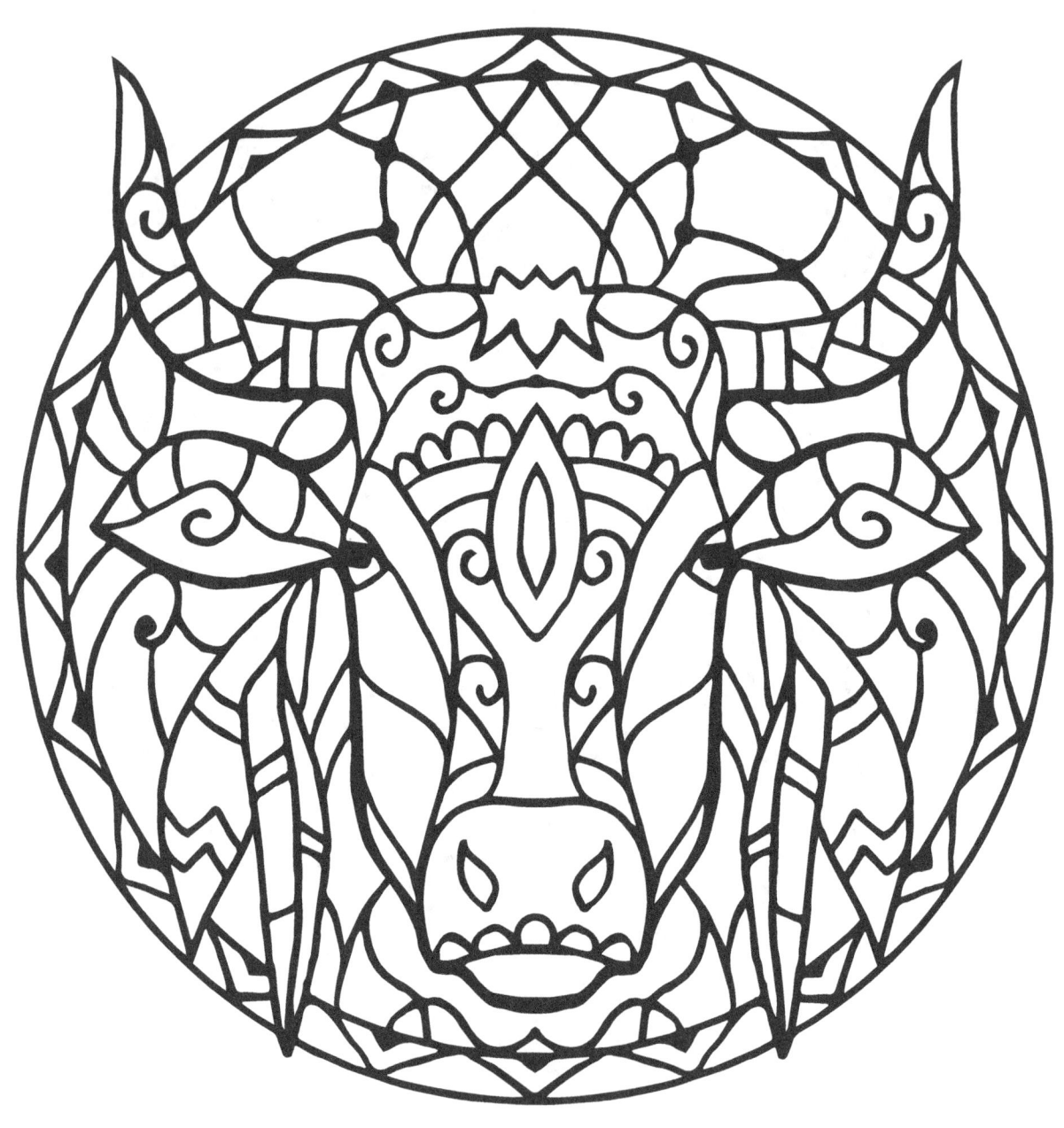

The Bull is considered a symbol of plentifulness and peace. Attributed as a symbol of strength, the Bull is often associated with divine masculinity and vigor.

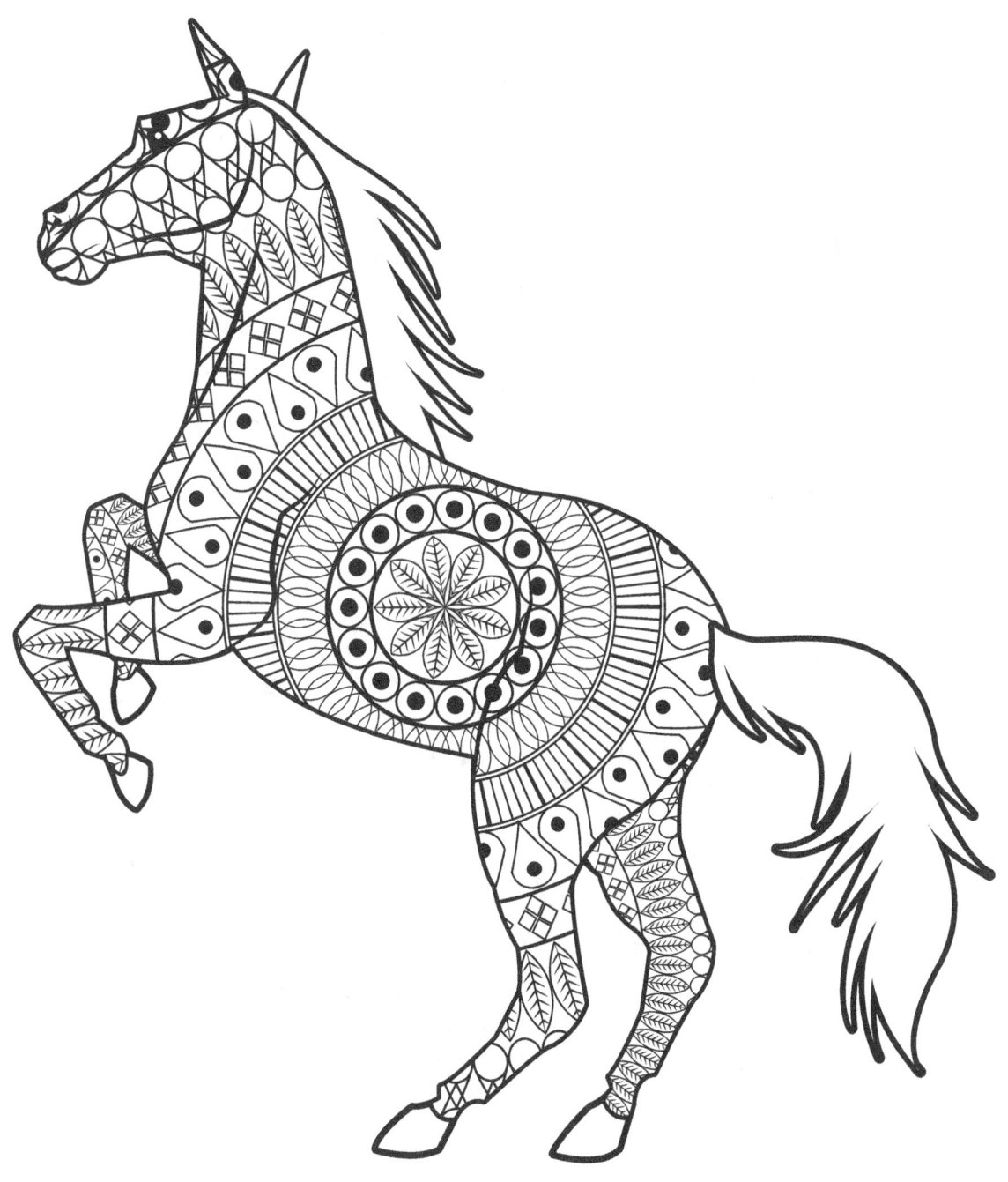

The Unicorn is a symbol of purity. Further as a symbol of optimism and enchantment, the Unicorn is magical, mythiical creature.

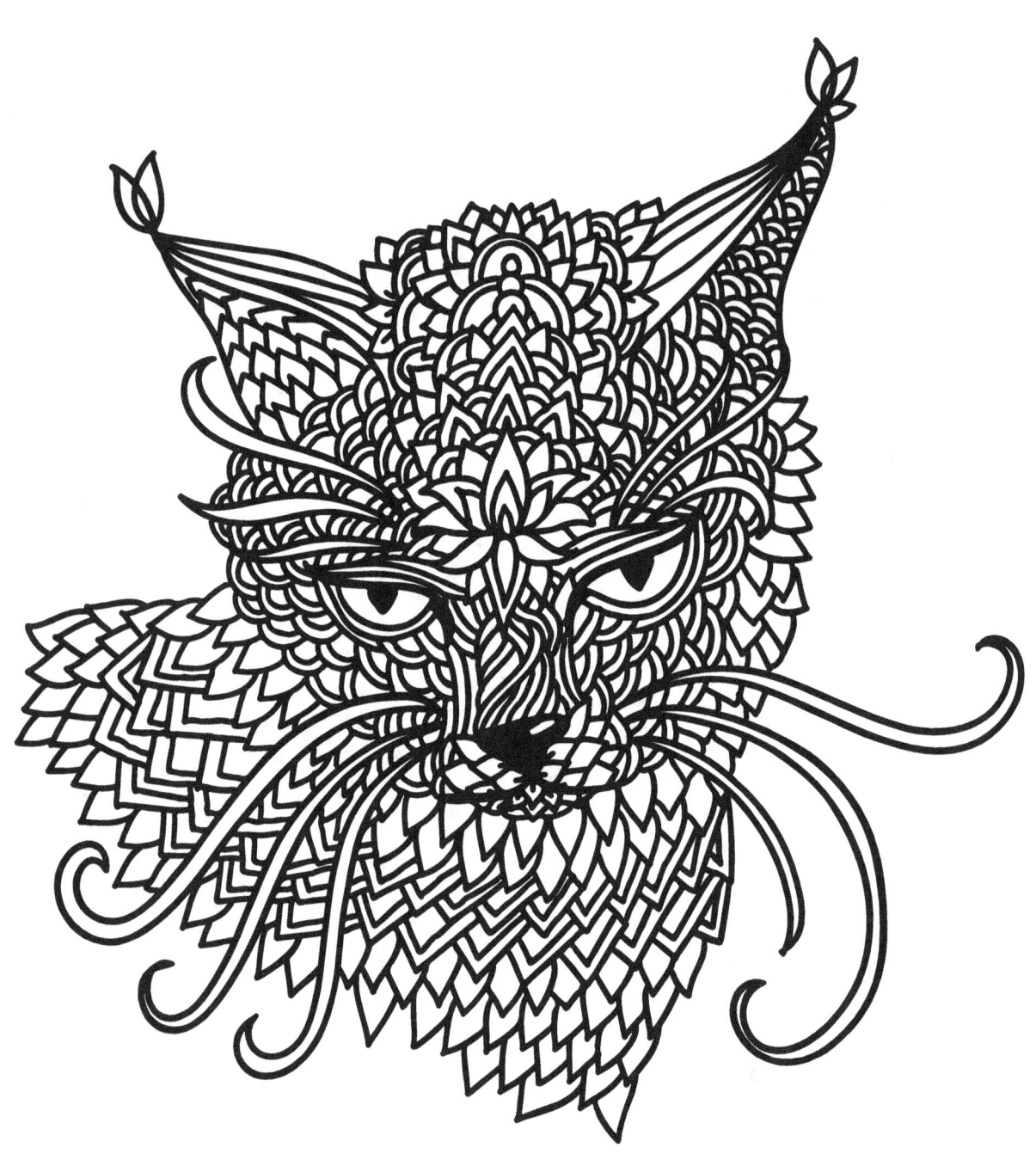

As a symbol of the spiritual world the cat signifies rebirth and reincarnation as well as growth of the soul.

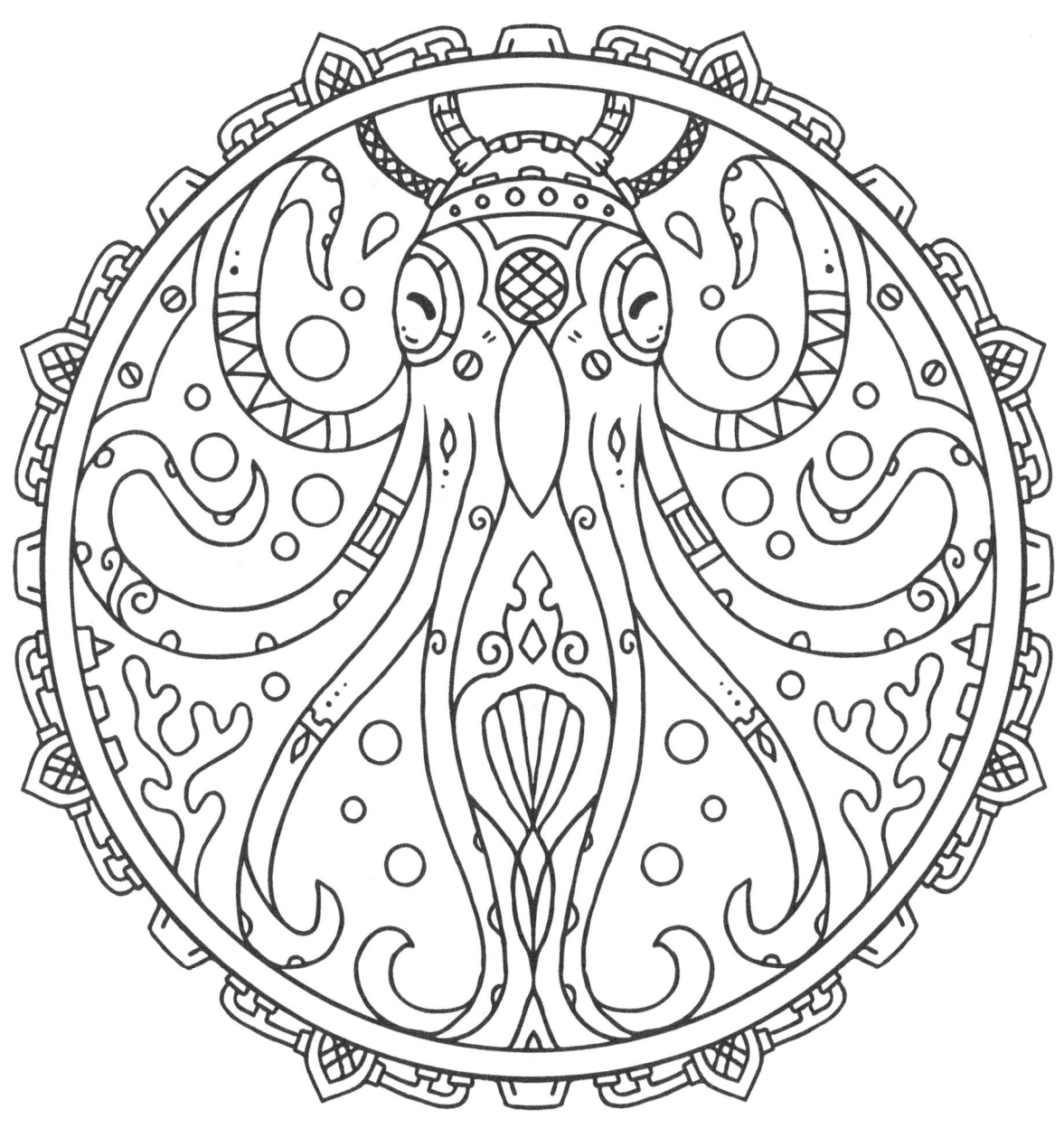

The Octopus is courageous and cunning. Symbolically, they embody focus, empowerment, and support.

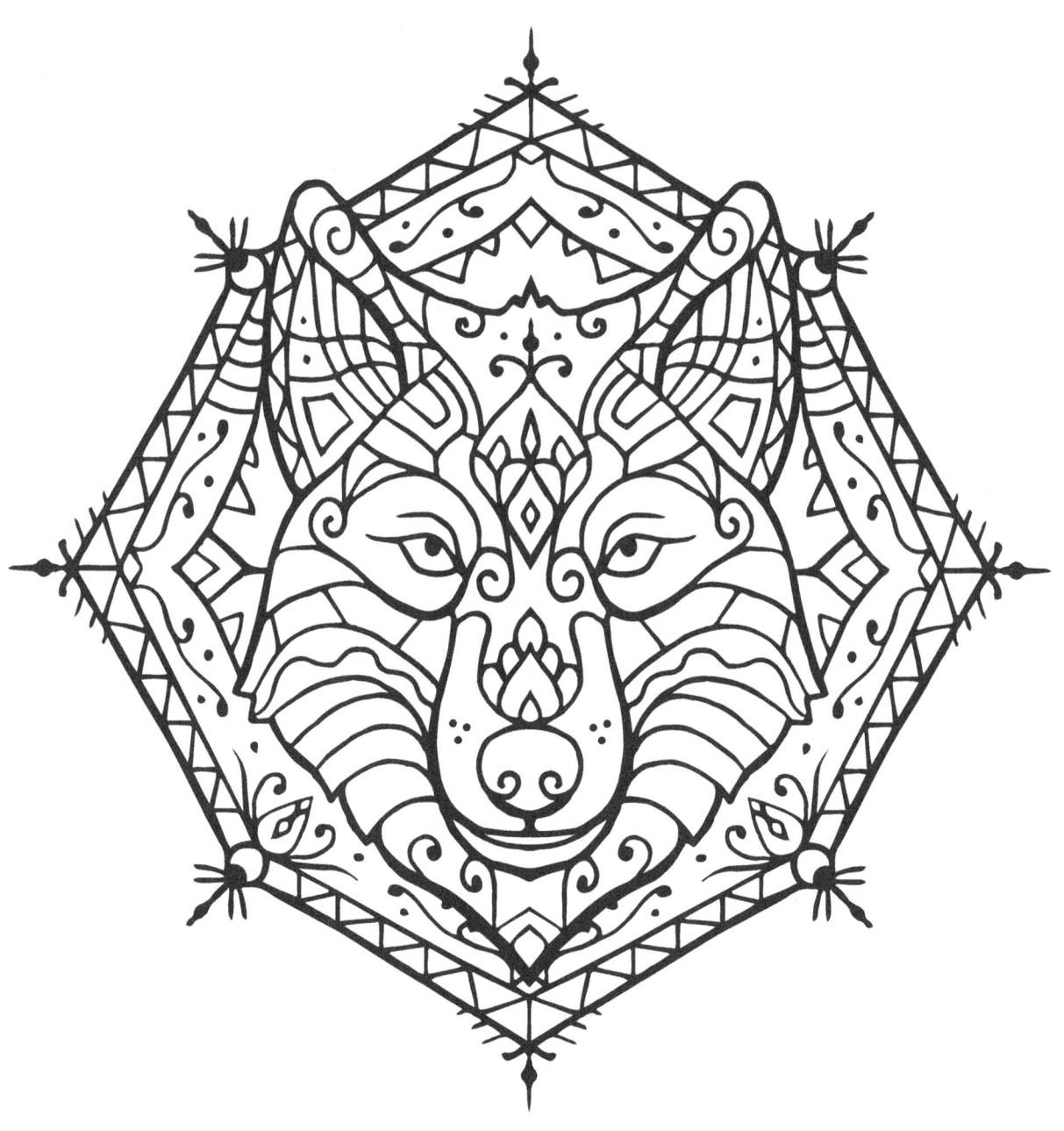

As an excellent hunter the Wolf can symbolize a call to take further look for deeper meaning while trusting our intuitive side.

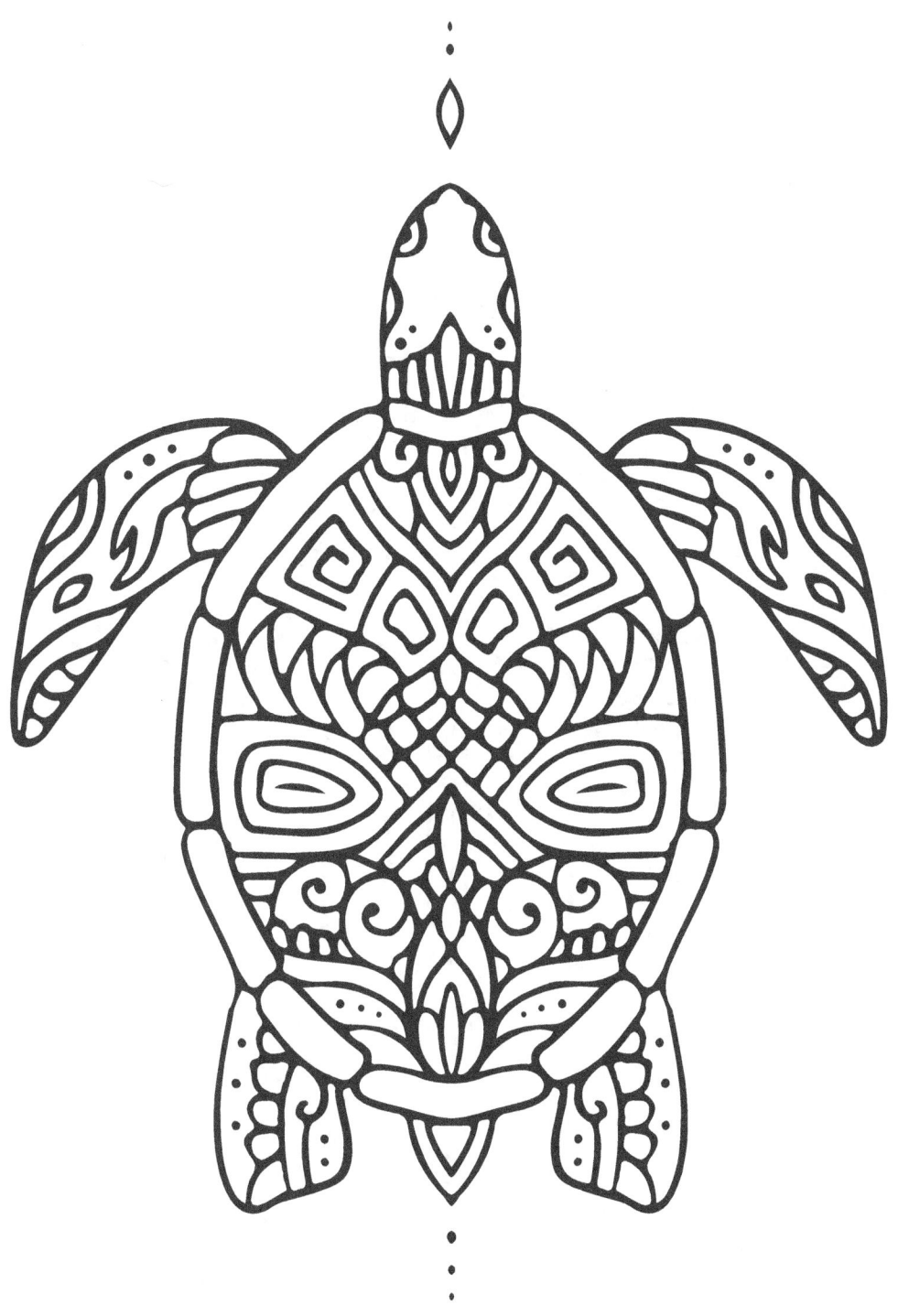

The Tortoise is known as a symbol of protection during life's journey. Often the Tortoise is associated with patience and vision.

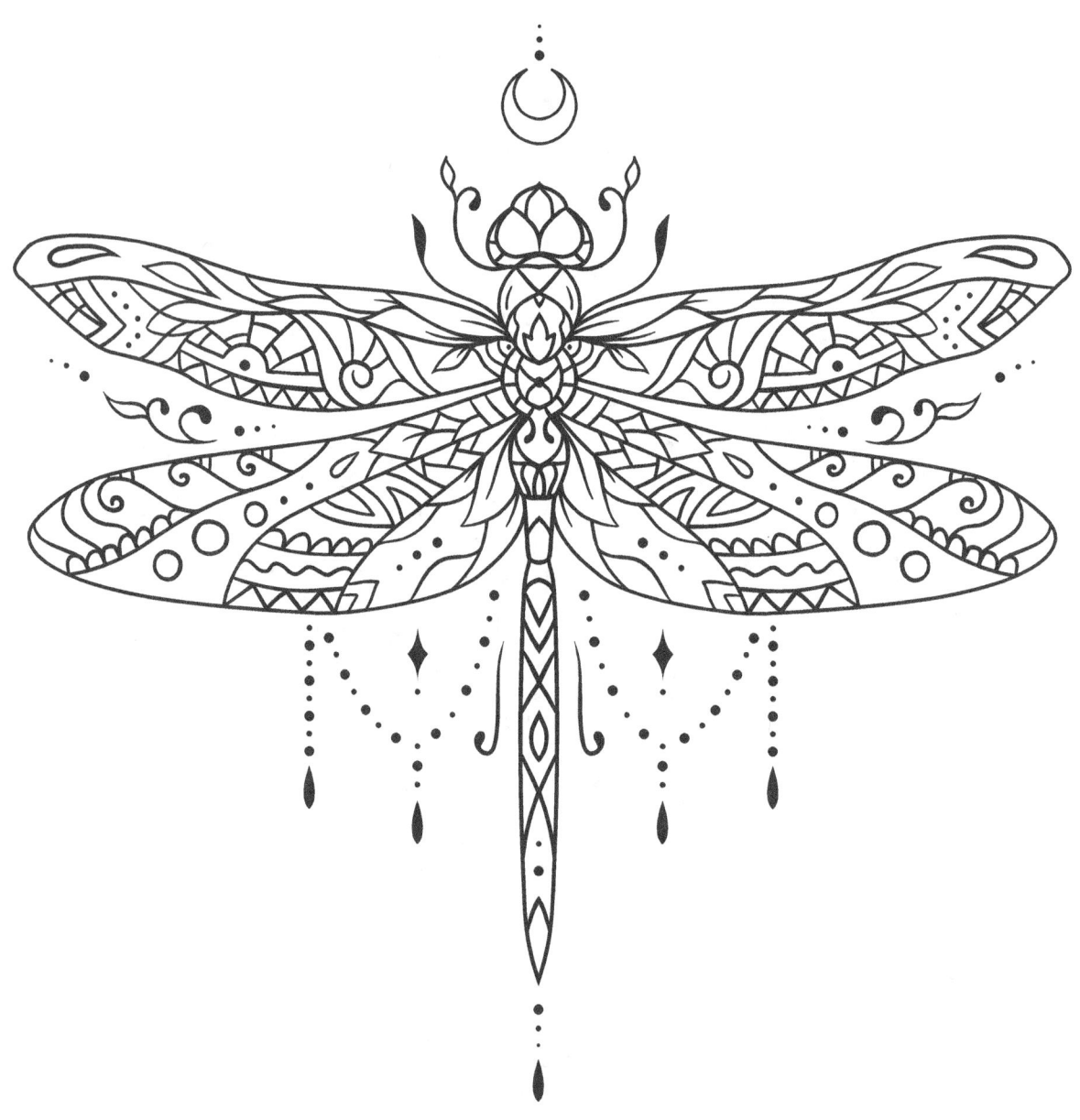

The Dragonfly symbolizes potential and transformation. The Dragonfly can be sign of a spiritual message inviting a new realm and state of mind.

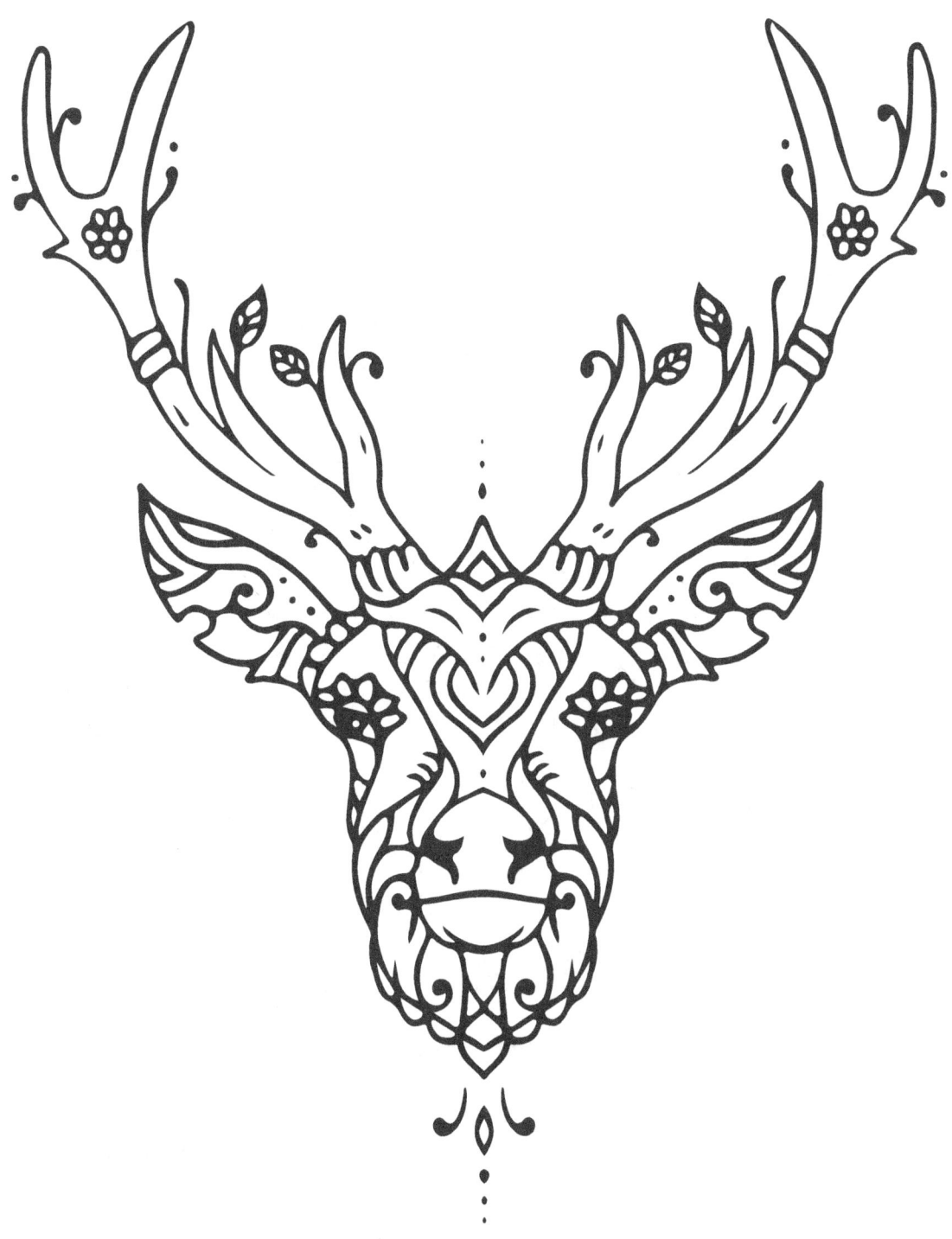

The Deer symbolizes the call to care for those that have been hurt. Deer embody gentleness and compassion.

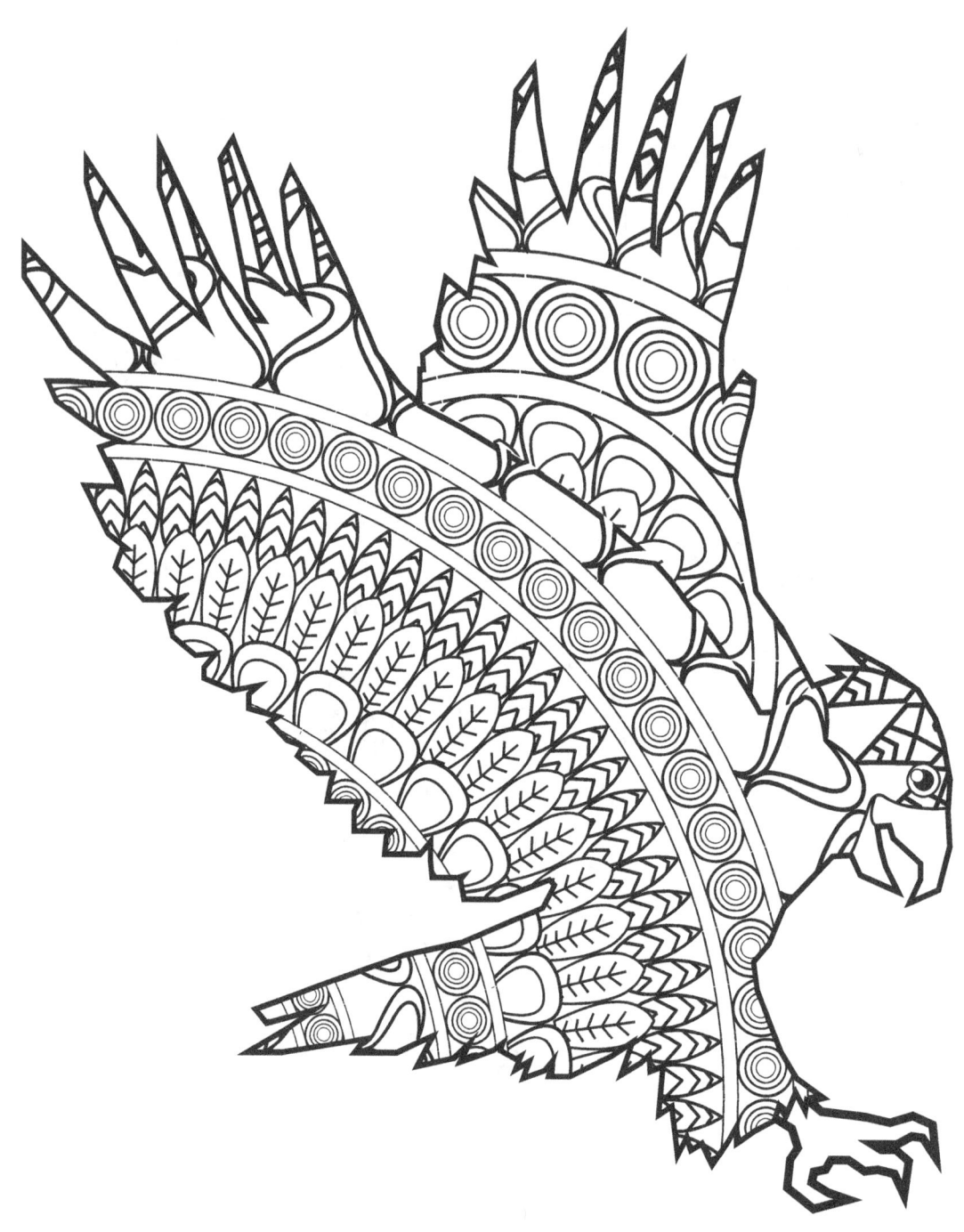

The Eagle is a symbol of change and renewal. The Eagle spirit animal represents fortitude and vision.

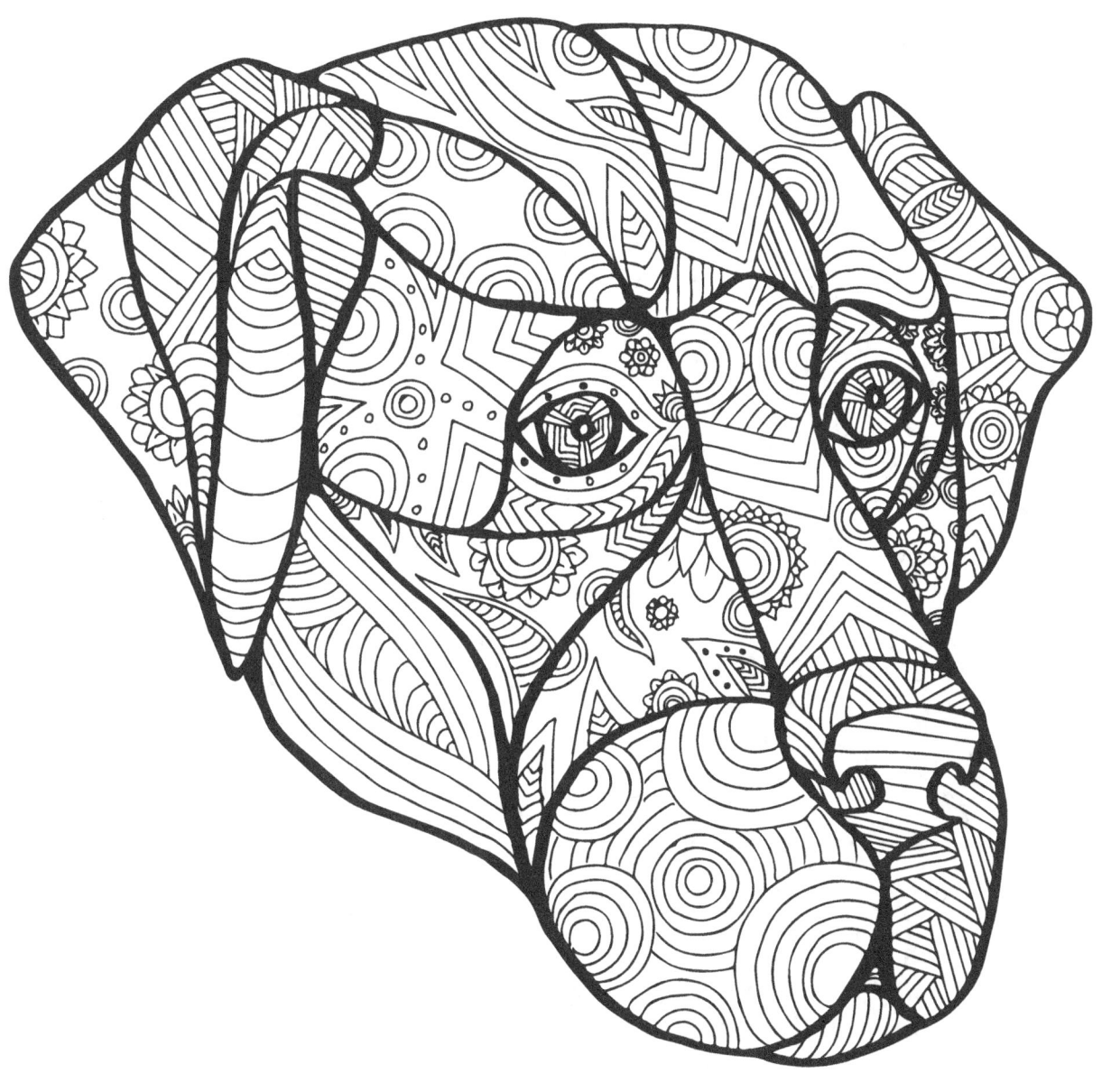

The Dog is a symbol of compassion and loyalty. Often called Man's best friend the dog embodies the spirit of cooperation, protection, and guidance in the afterlife.

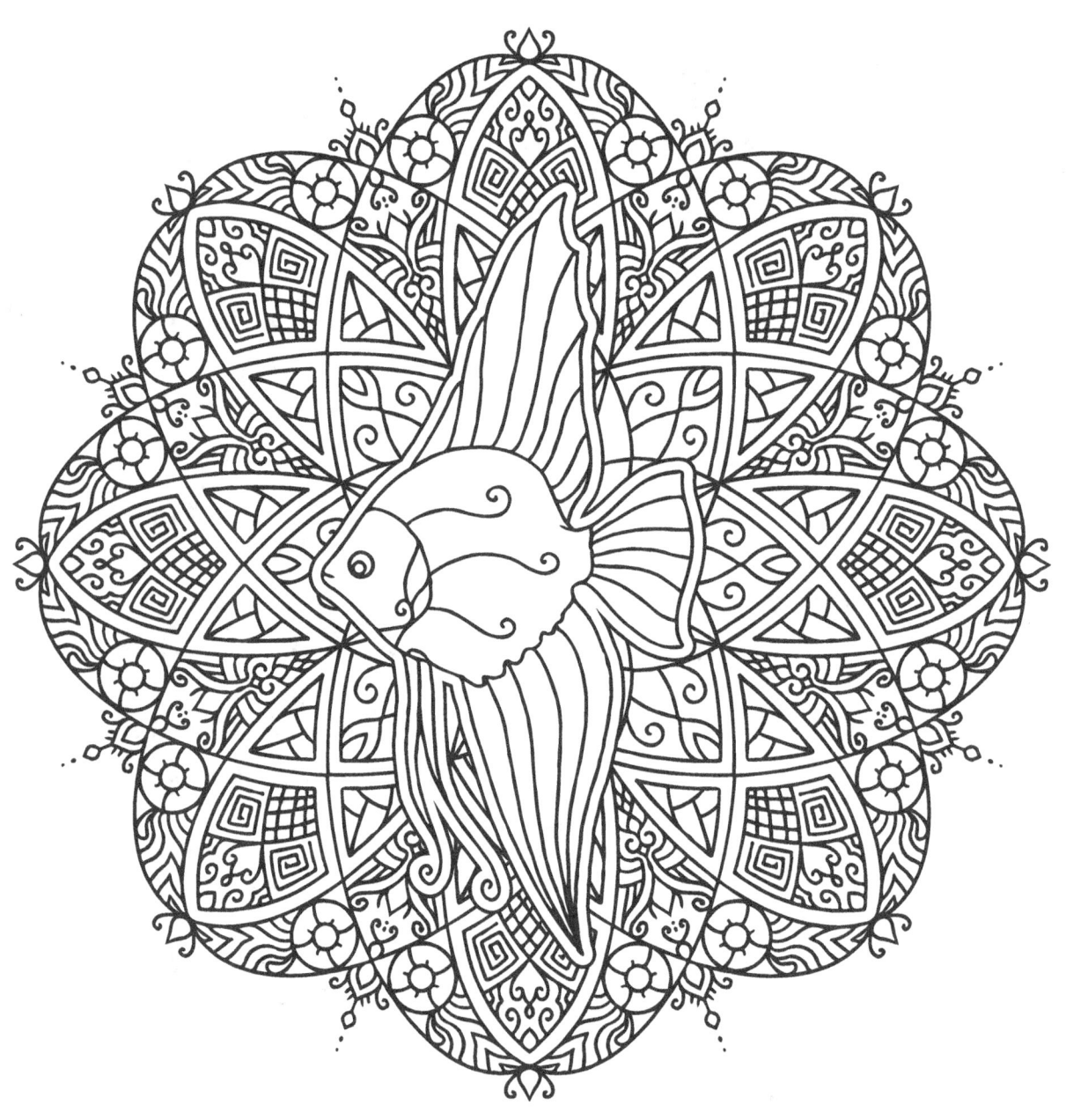

The Fish represents understanding of the spiritual self. As a symbol of joy, longevity and plentifulness the fish has religious significance for many.

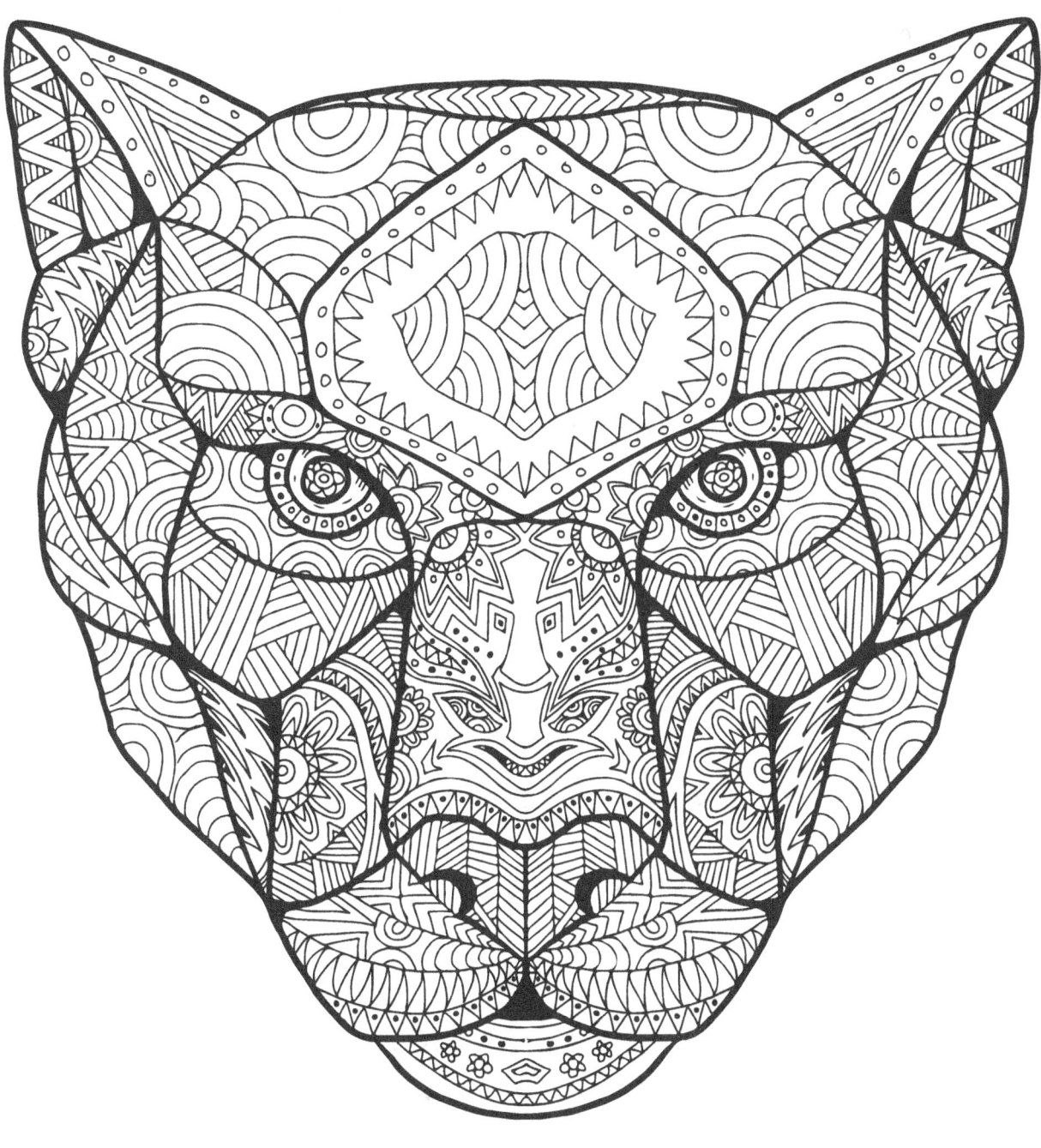

The Panther signifies intuition, awareness, and protection. As guardian and fierce hunter the panther embodies power and insight during times of darkness.

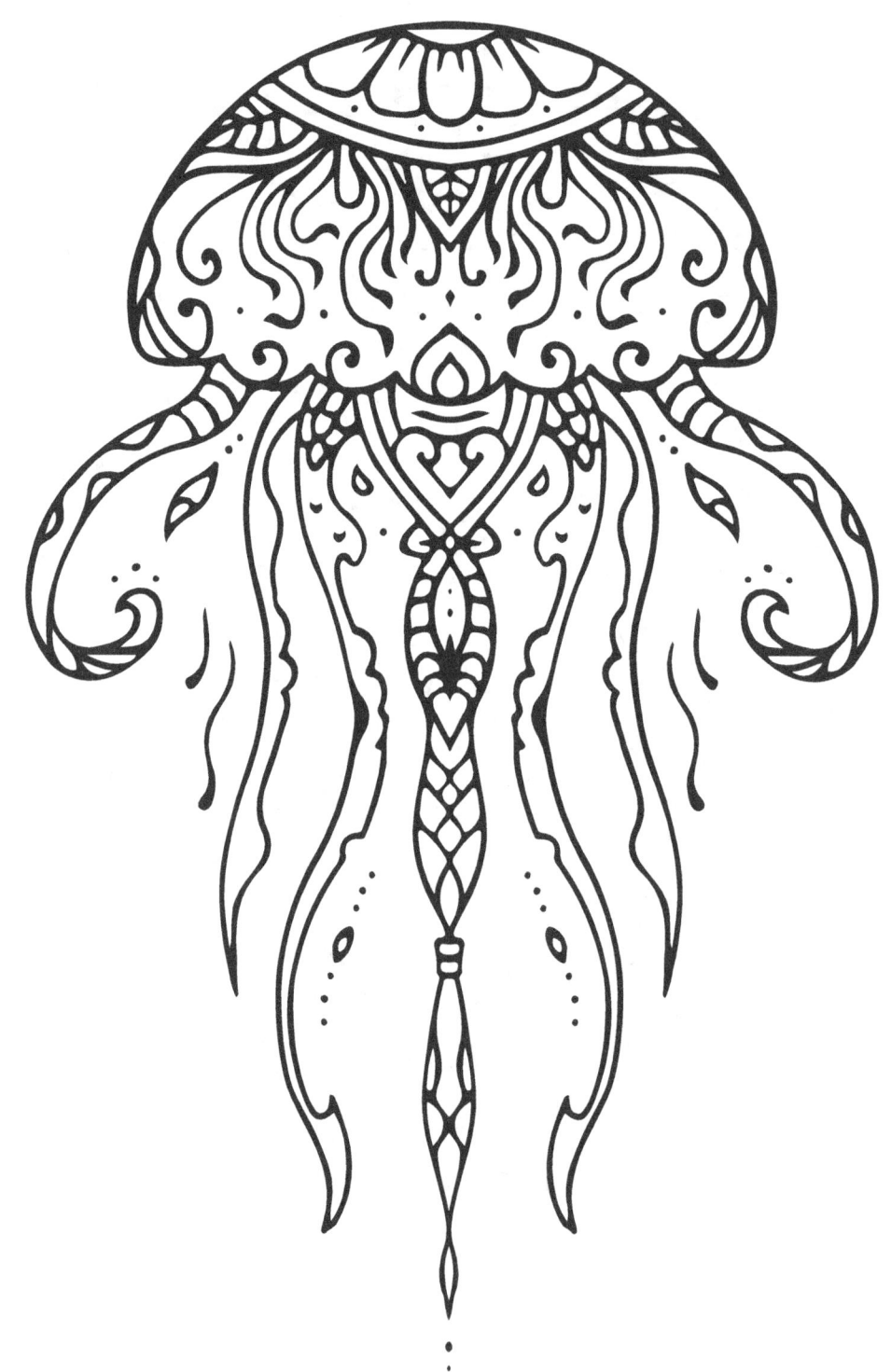

Jellyfish are said to be messengers. As symbol of teaching and tranquility the jellyfish embodies a calm force reminding to stay at peace.

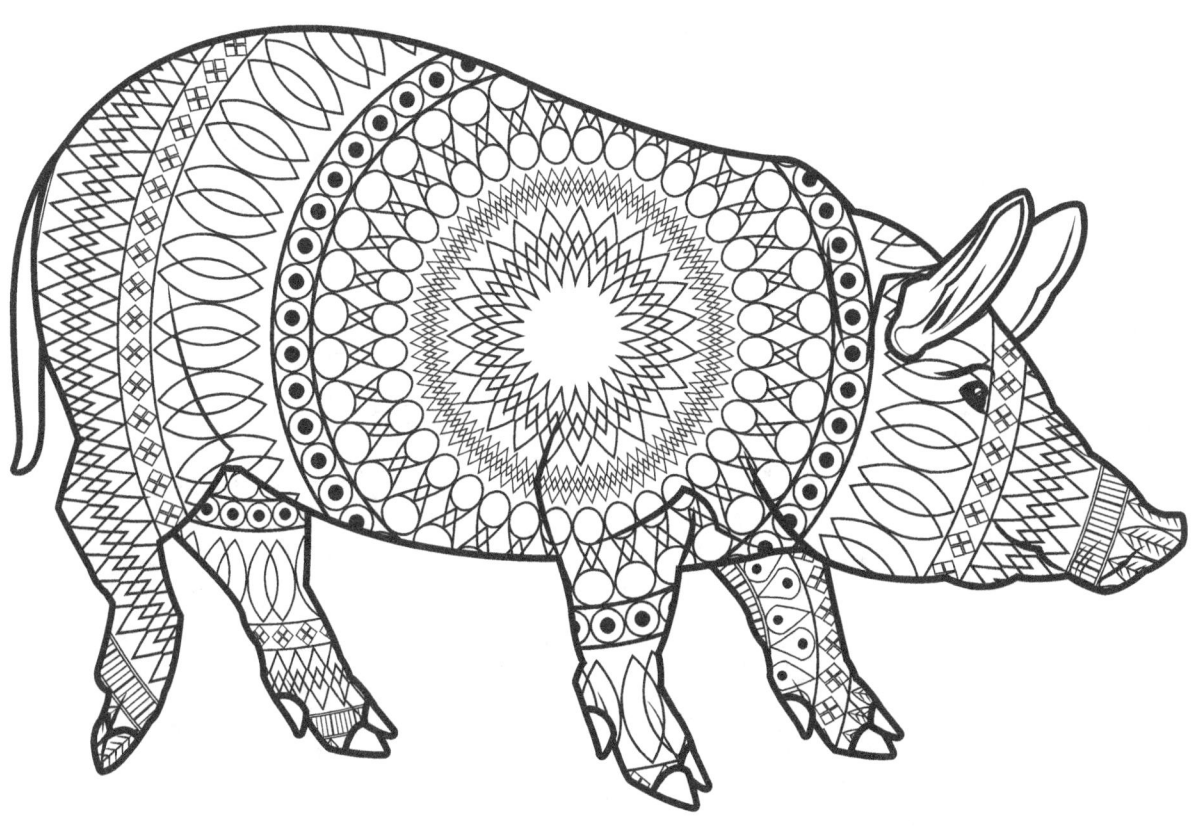

The Pig is a symbol of high intellect but is also a symbol of caution regarding obliviousness to greed and egotism.

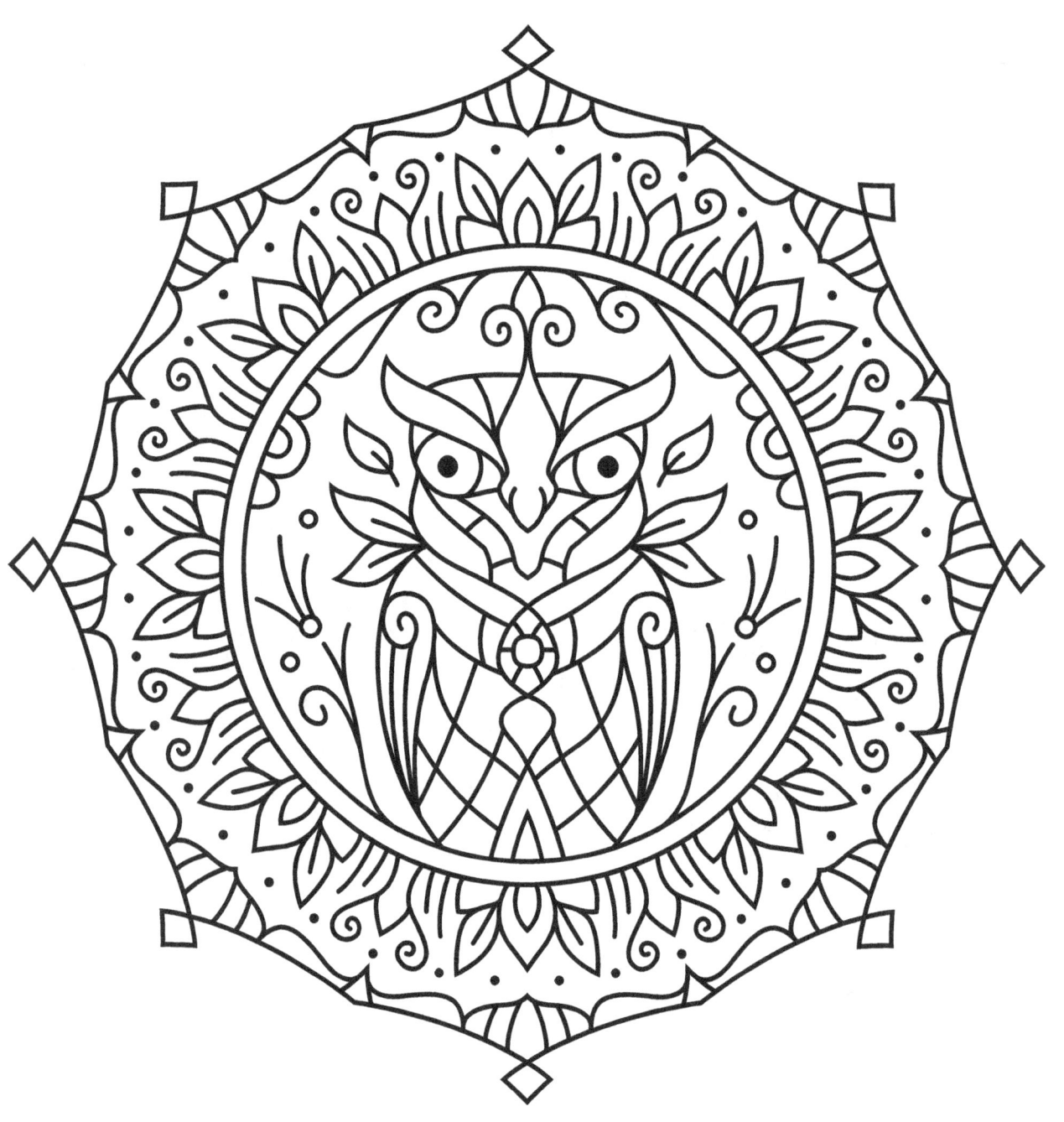

The Owl has been considered a spiritual messenger from ancient times and is a symbol of trust, prophecy, and a reminder of strength and wisdom in challenging times.

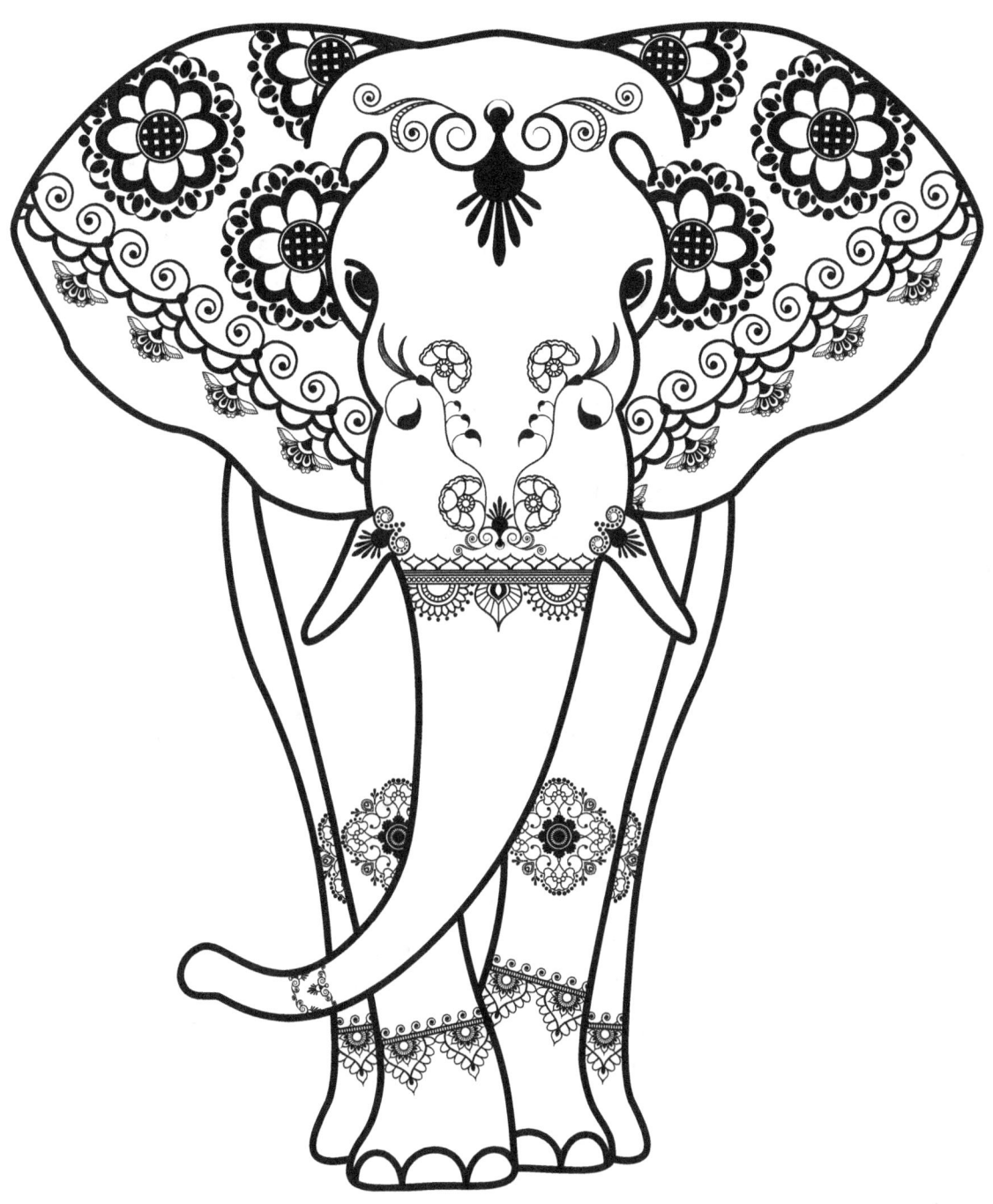

The Elephant is a symbol of compassion and purity. The saying goes Elephants never forget thus the elephant embodies intelligence and patience.

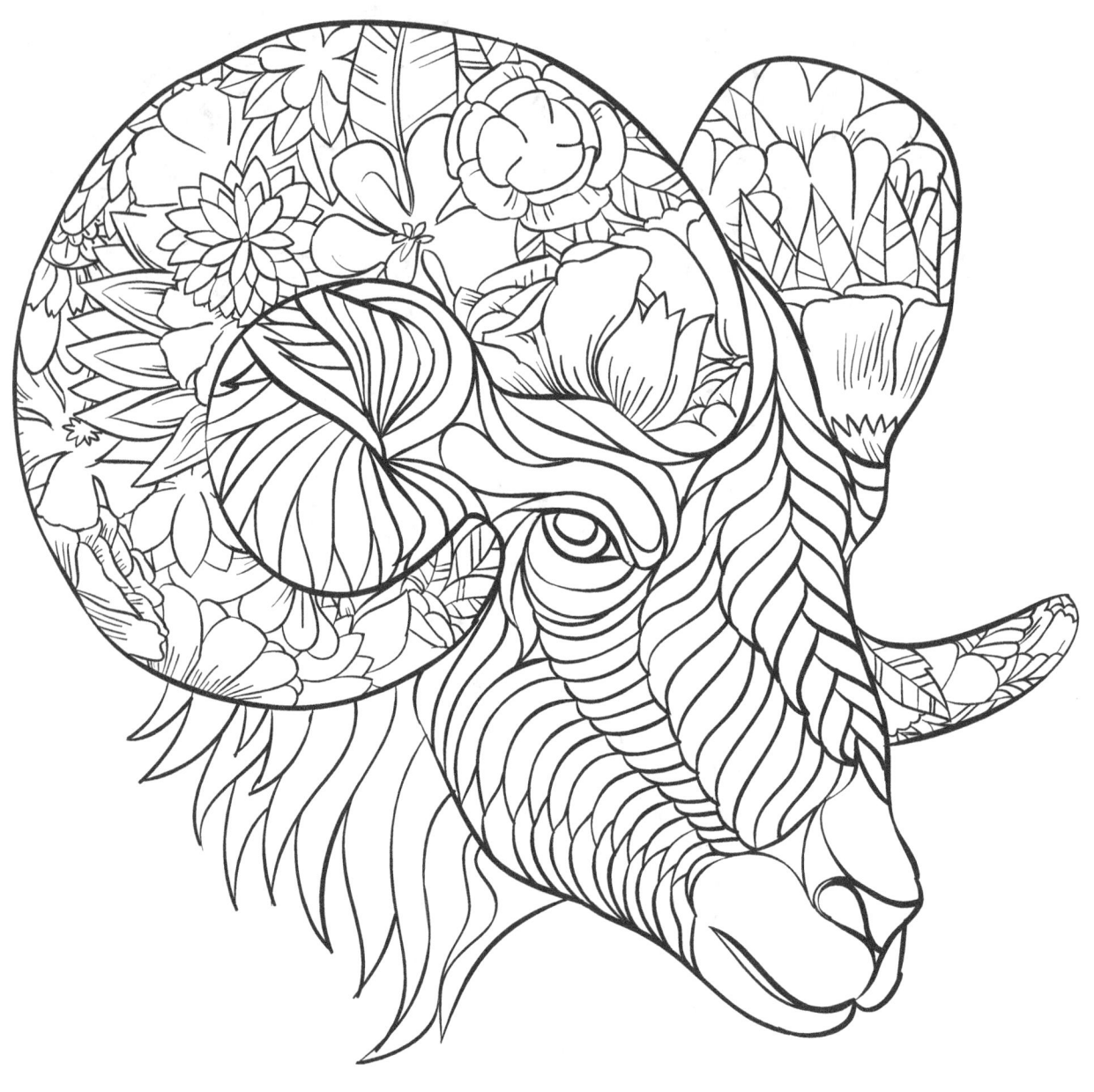

The Ram represents wise calculation and intuition. Courage is embodied in the Ram aswell as noble discernment.

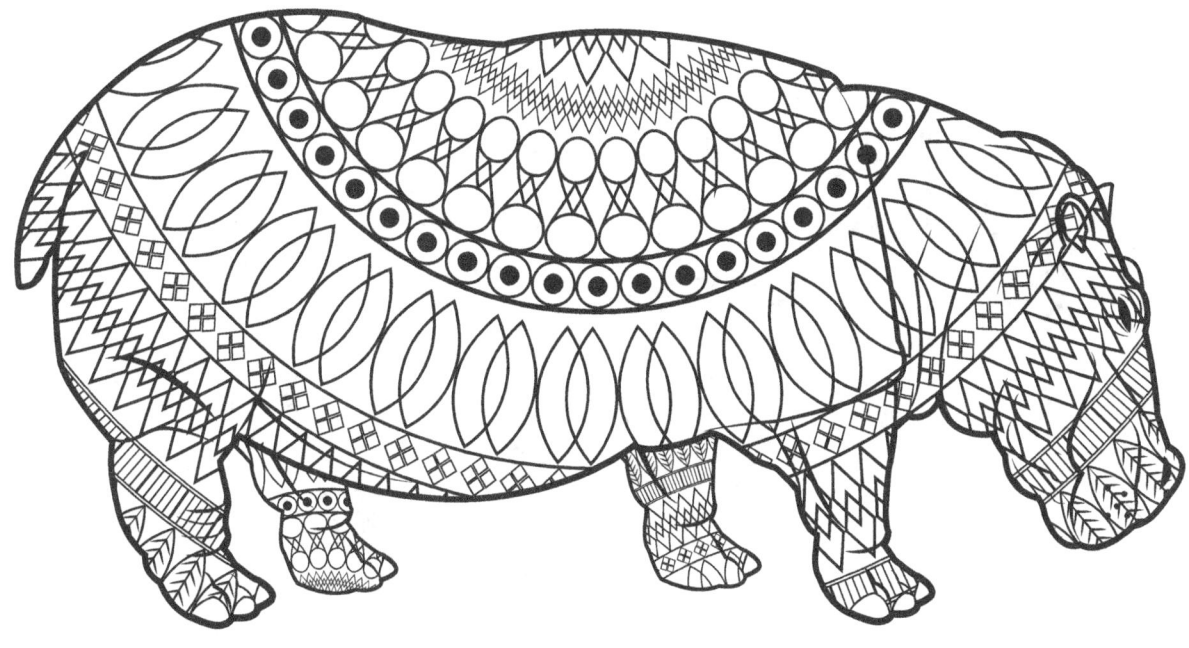

The Hippopotamus, also known as the water horse, signifies healing and imagination and protection through our Mothers.

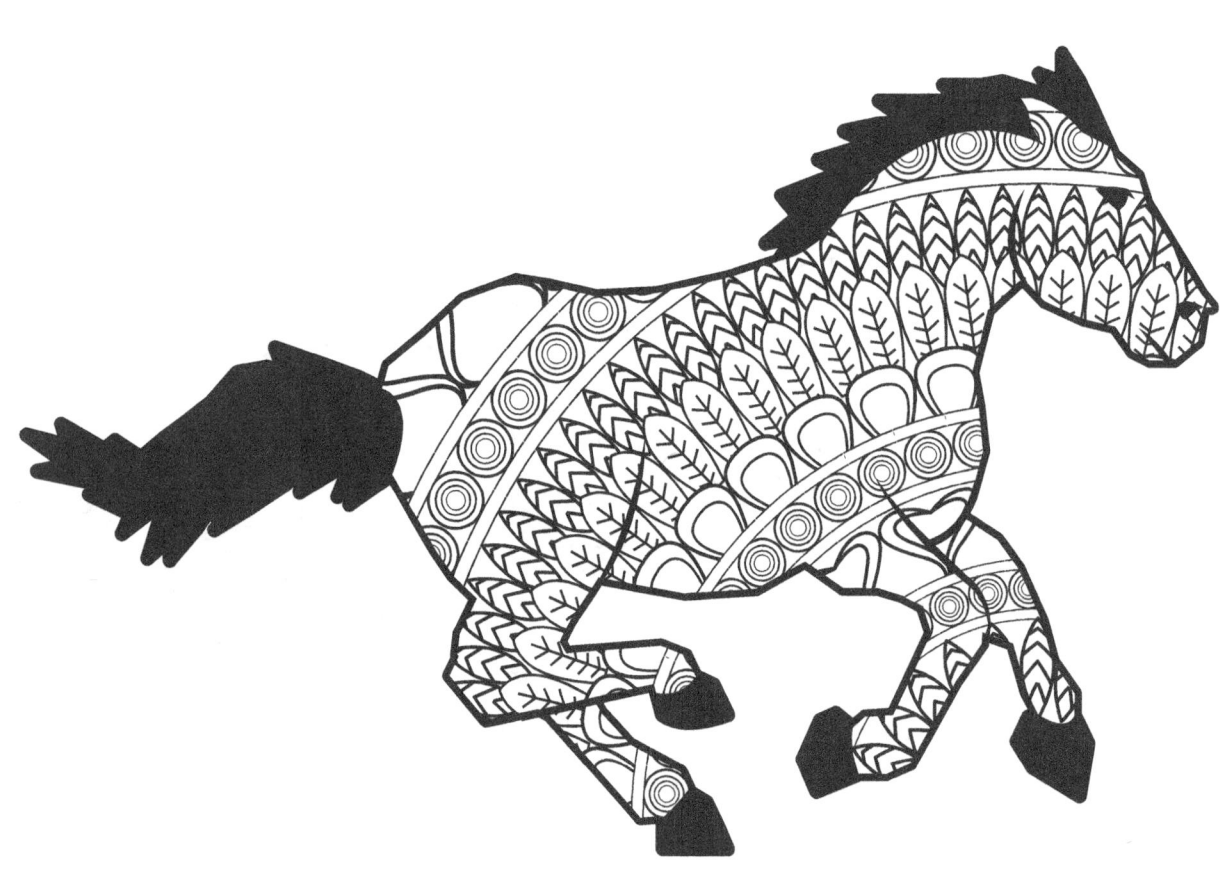

The Horse is a symbolizes forces of nature in the elements. The Horse spirit signifies spontaneity, passion, and freedom.

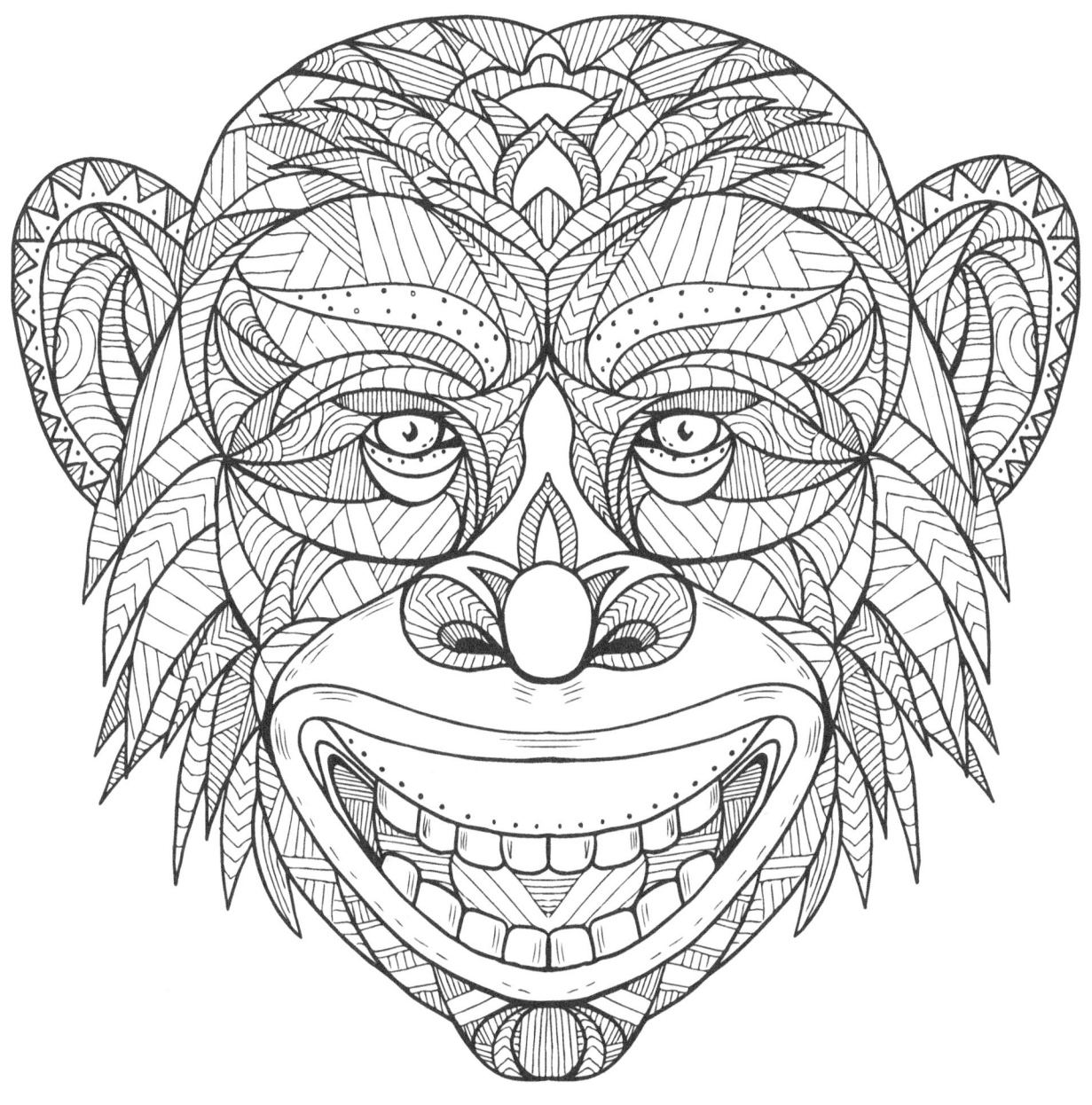

The Monkey symbolizes charm, understanding and friendship. In some cultures, based on the color, the monkey foretells generosity and divine protection.

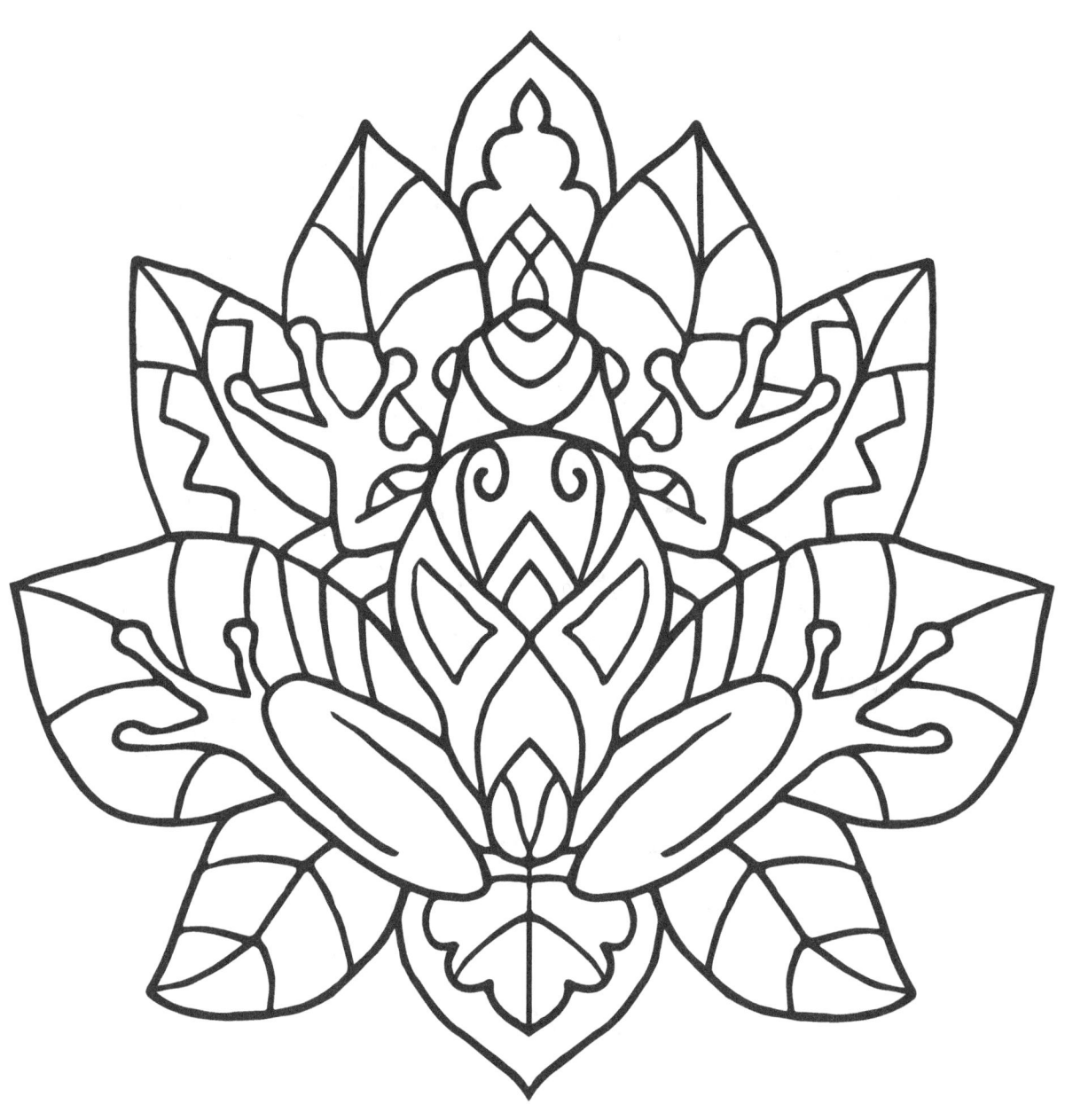

The frog represents protection of children and fertility. In some cultures the frog is very important to the cosmic creation of the universe as well as representing renewal and introspection.

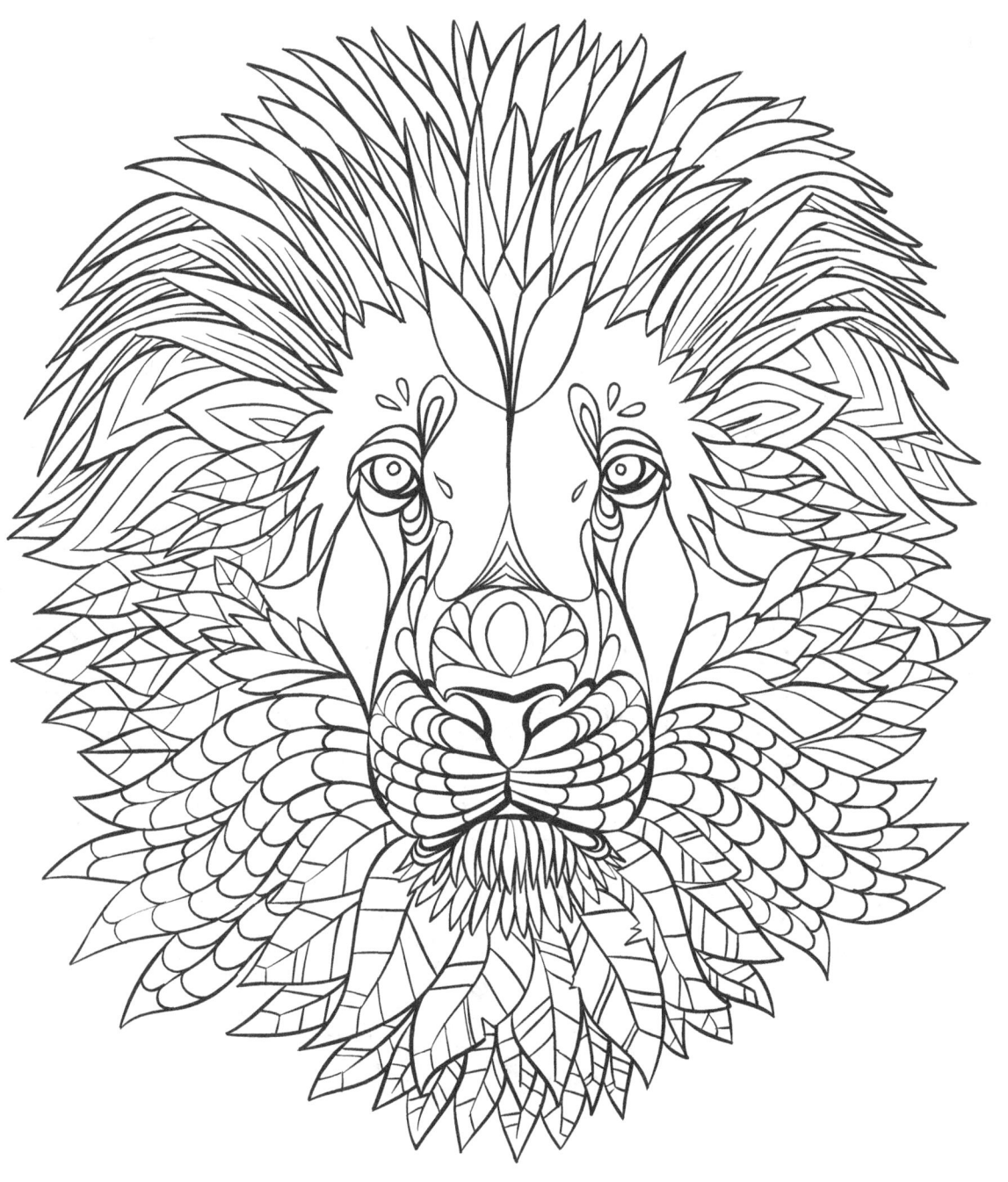

The Lion is often a symbol of the sun. As a symbol of the sage the lion can represent knowledge of natural instincts, ruthlessness, and the divine sovereignty .

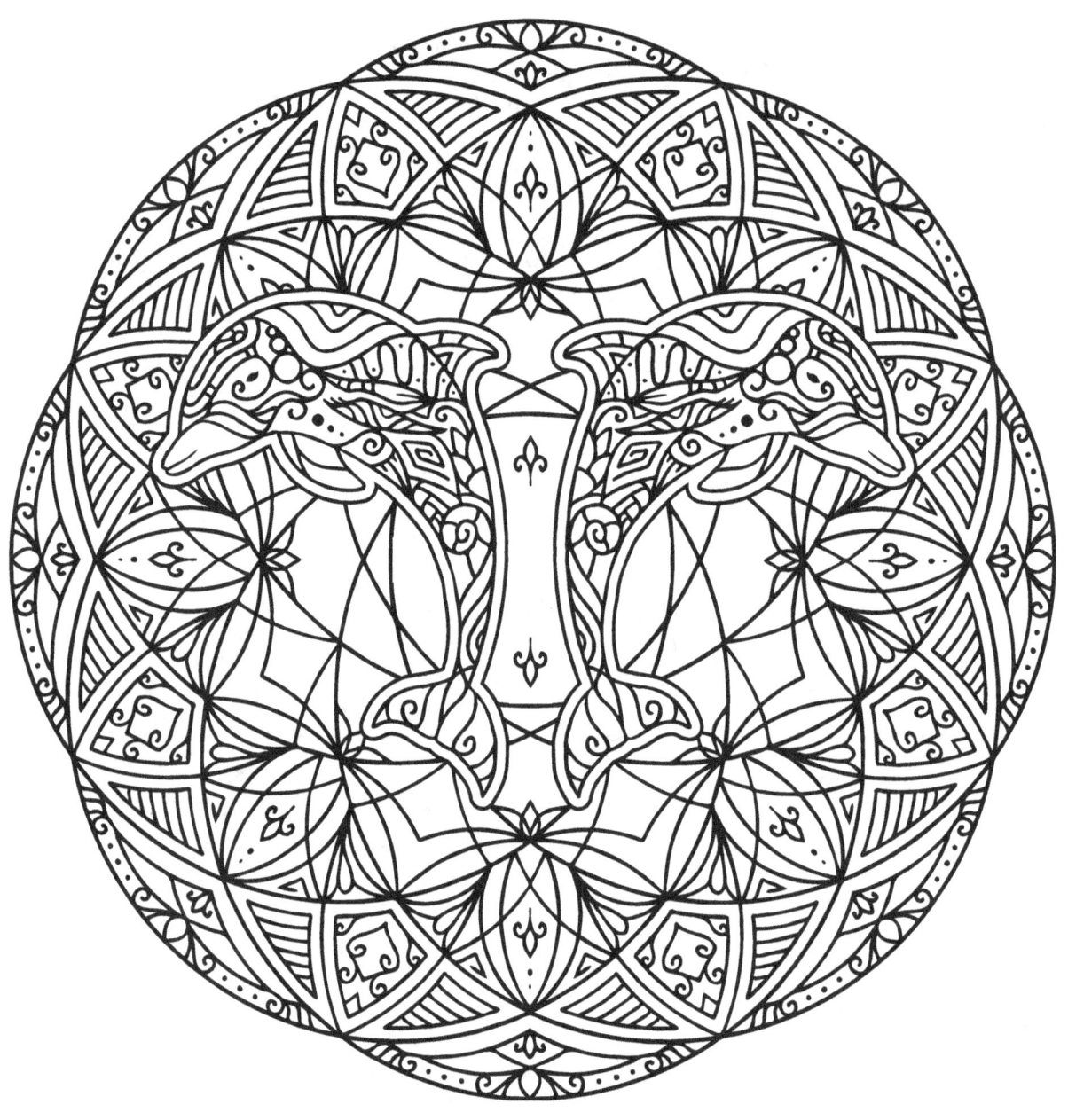

The Dolphin symbolizes grace and the relationship between the human family and nature. Sometimes the Dolphin is seen as a symbol of sacred femininity.

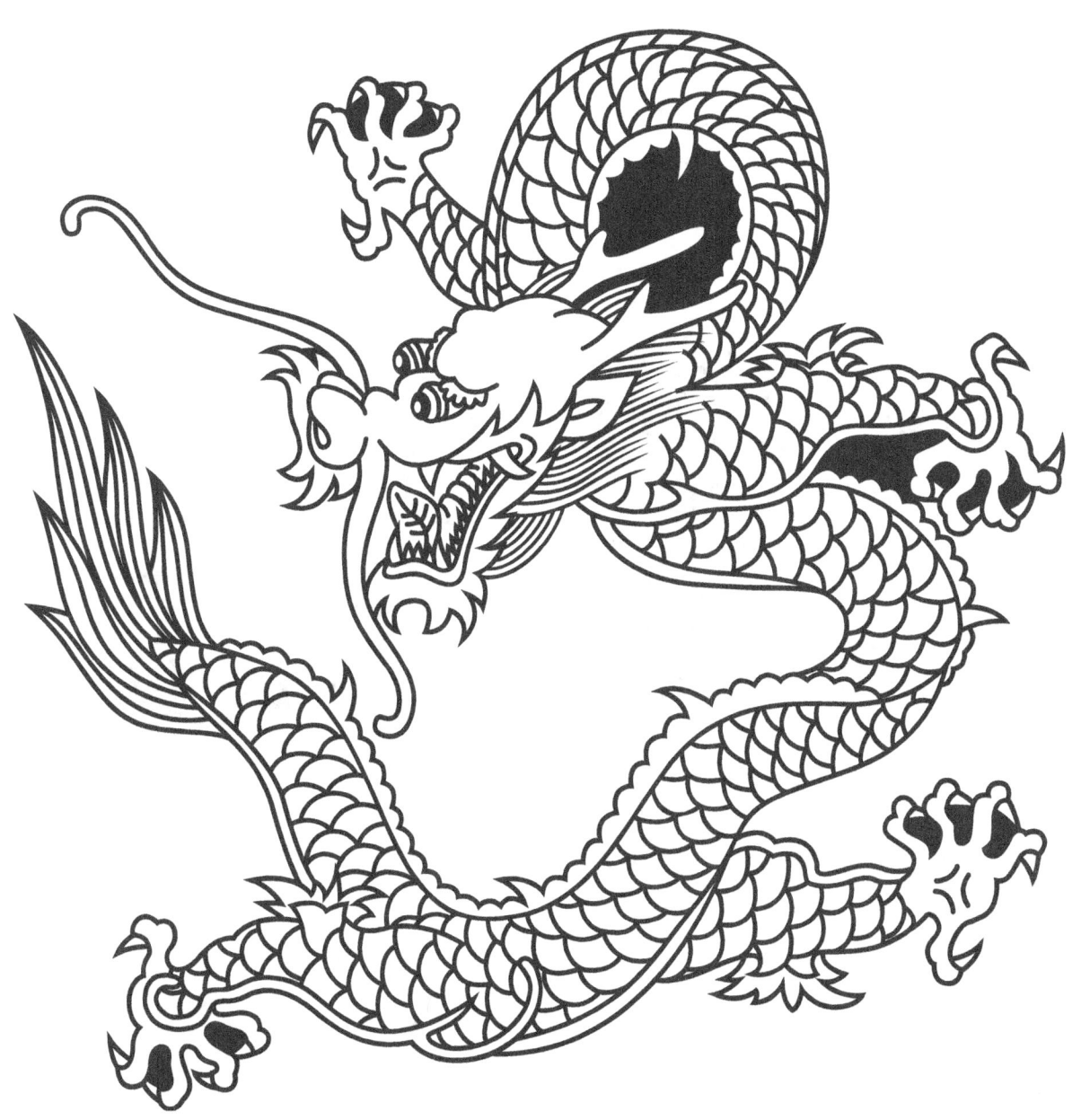

In mythology as magical and powerful creature, symbolically the Dragon is associated with cleverness, creativity, guidance and judgement.

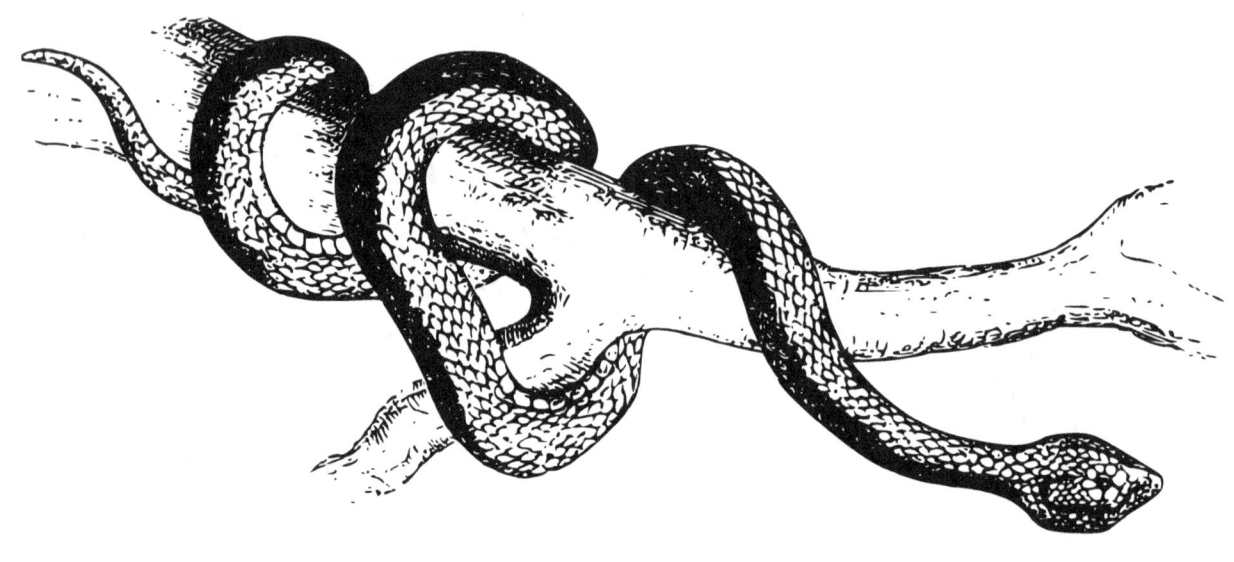

The Snake is a symbol of longevity and intelligence. In the snake we see a symbol of the eternal and unknown power of light and dark forces in nature and creation.

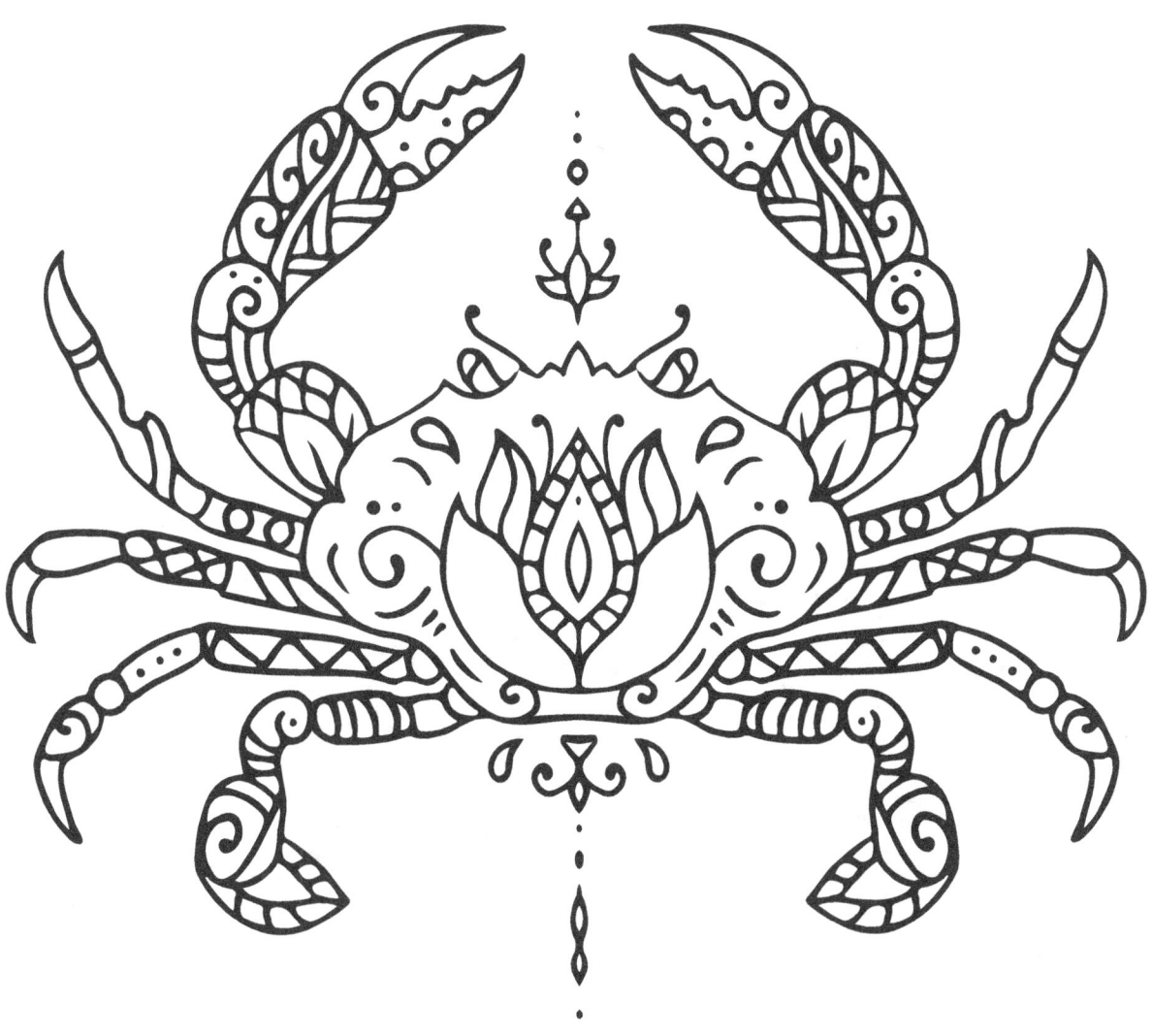

The Crab is a symbol of protection. The Crab reminds us to look at the direction of life and to trust while not letting emotions overwhelm our judgement.

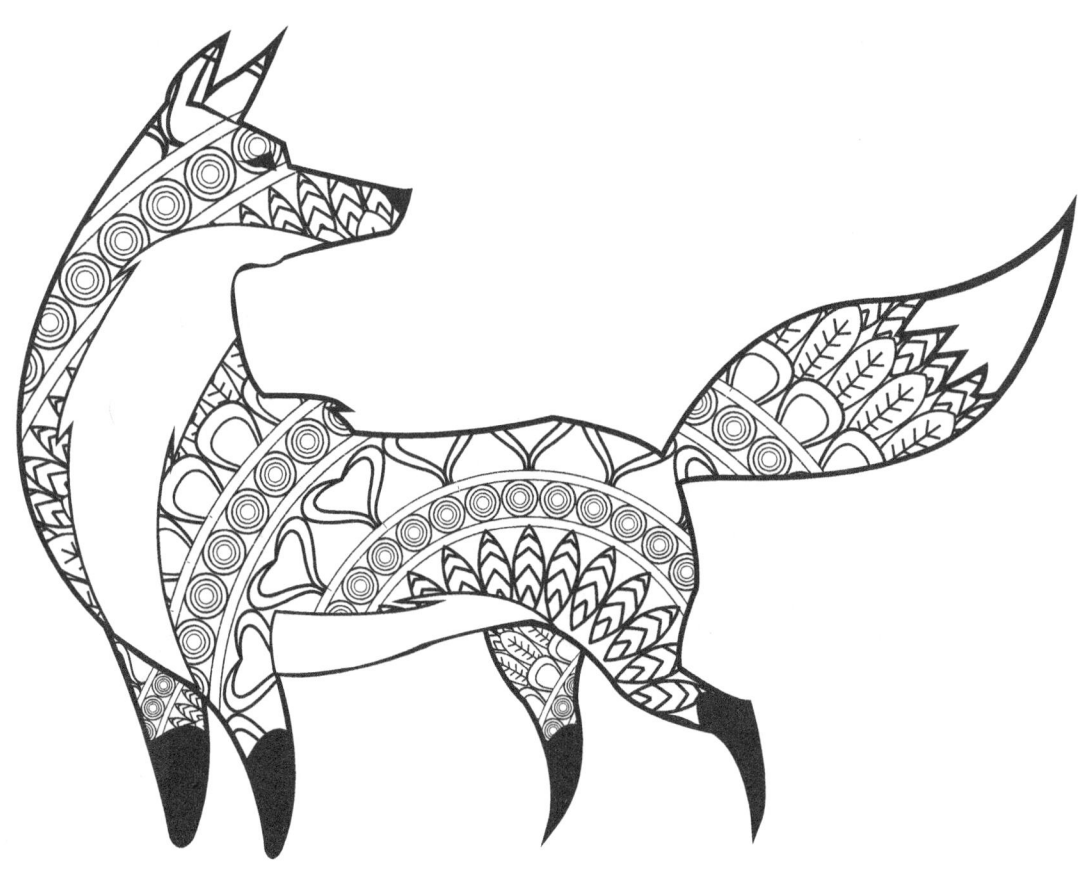

The fox is a symbol of purity and the divine forest. Foxes are thought to symbolize intelligence and the fertility of life.

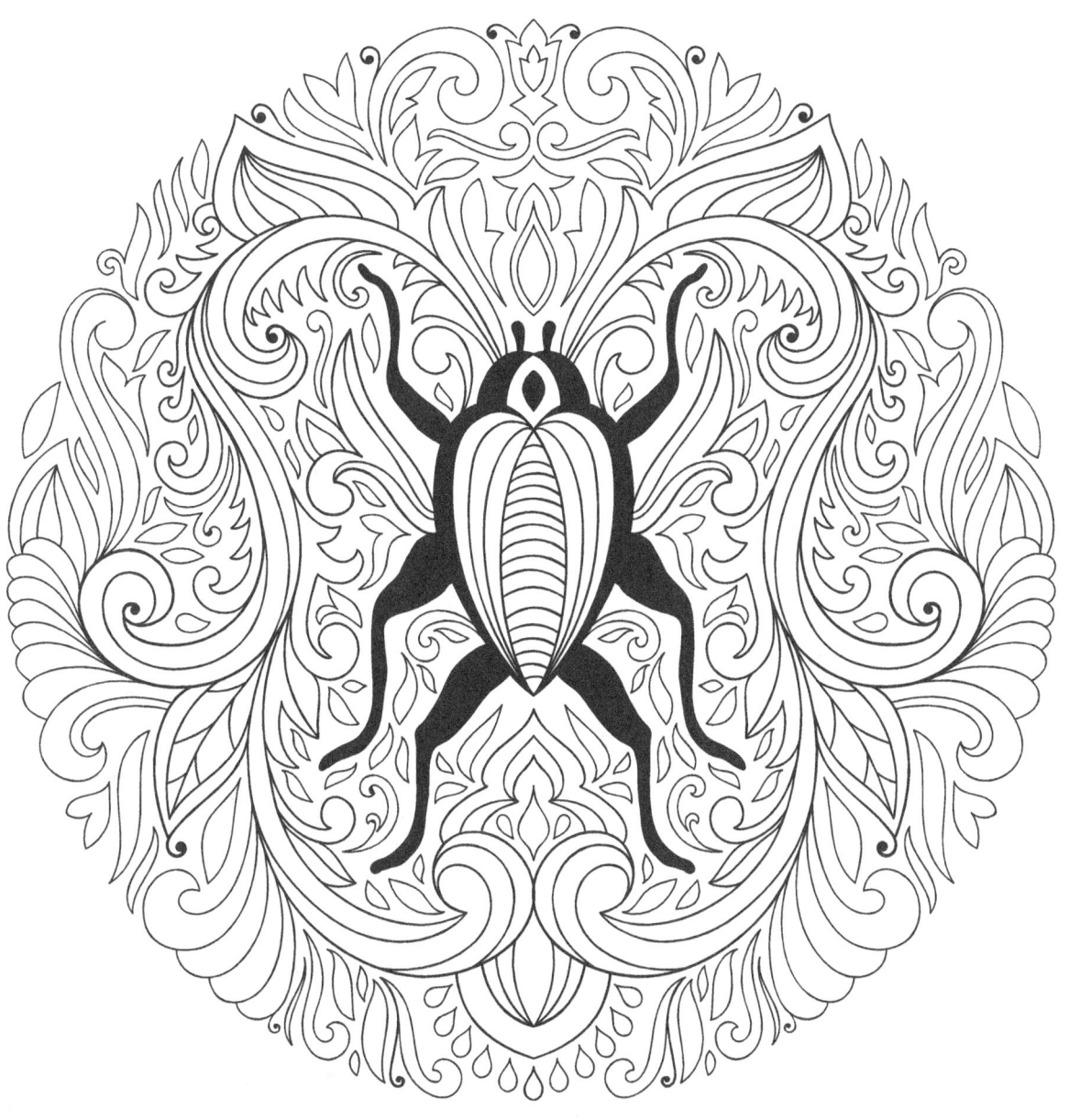

The Beetle is a symbol of love, dedication, and the willingness to compromise for the greater good. Symbolically the Beetle is associated with change and evaluation.

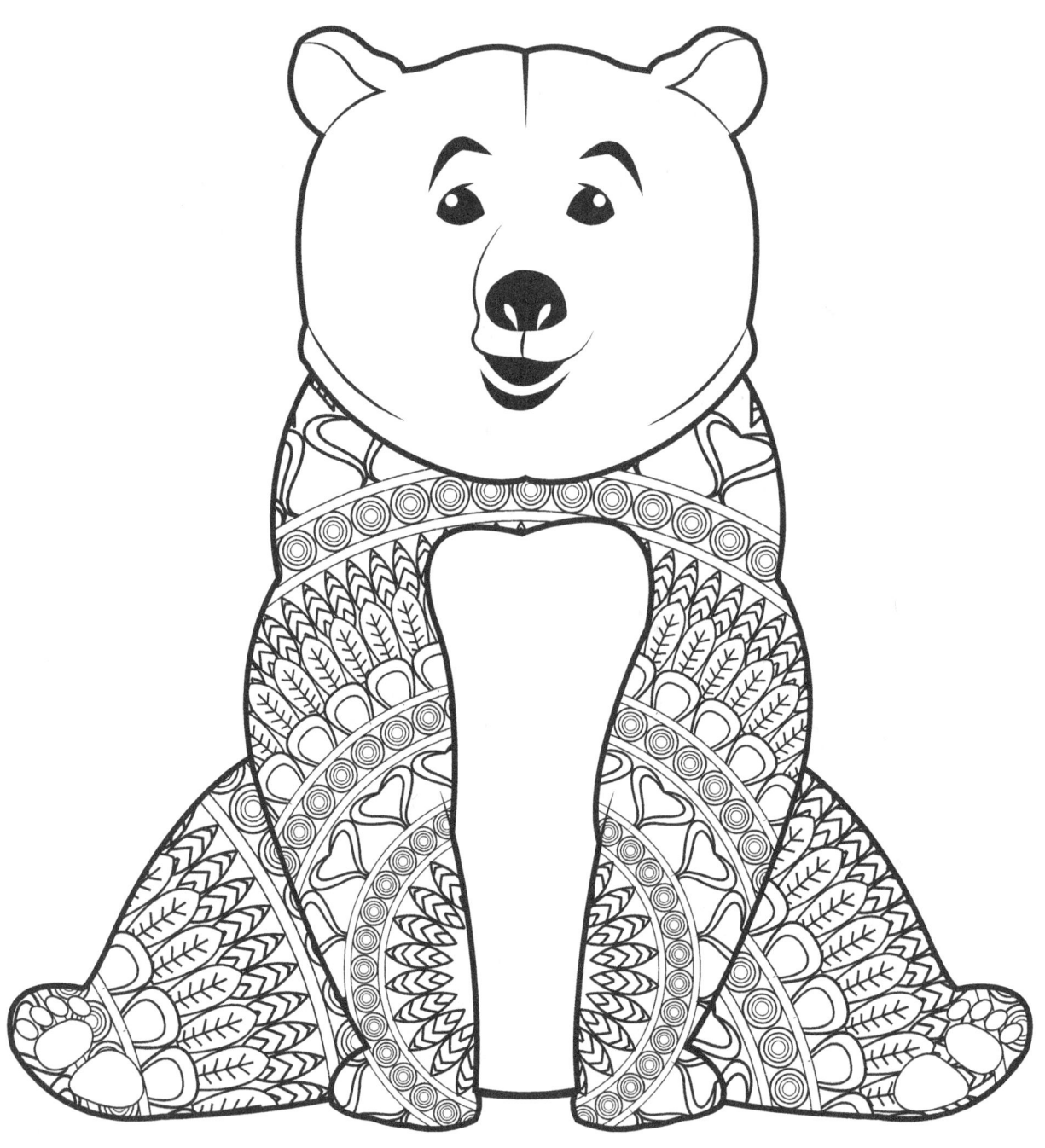

The Bear signifies holding fast to genuineness and truth. The bear symbolically embodies resurrection, self-healing, and steadfastness.

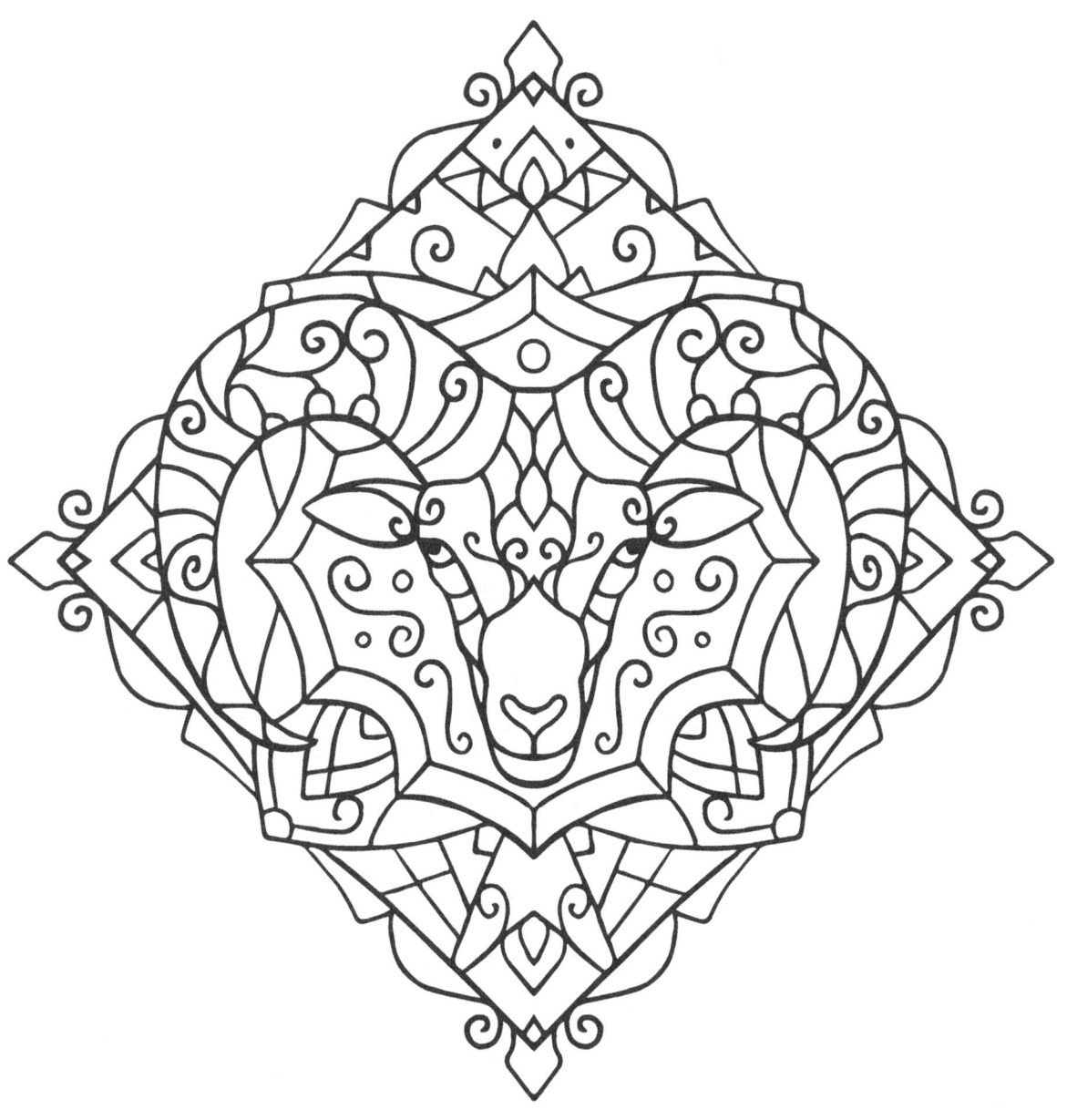

The Goat symbolizes sustenance and determination. Goats emblemize persistence and faith and sometimes hedonism.

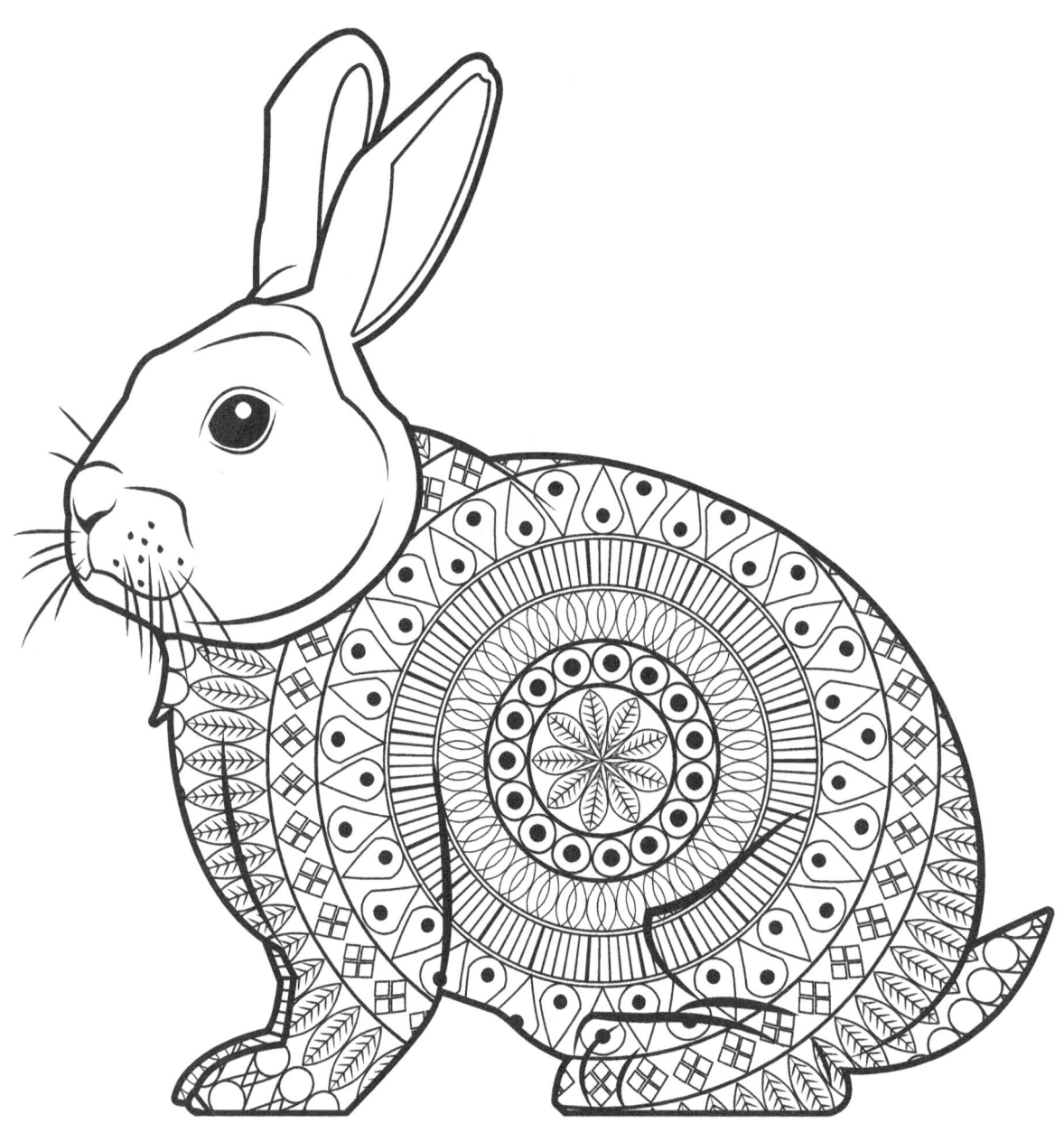

The Rabbit symbolizes wealth and abundance. The Rabbit reminds us to be healthy and is sometimes considered a symbol of seduction

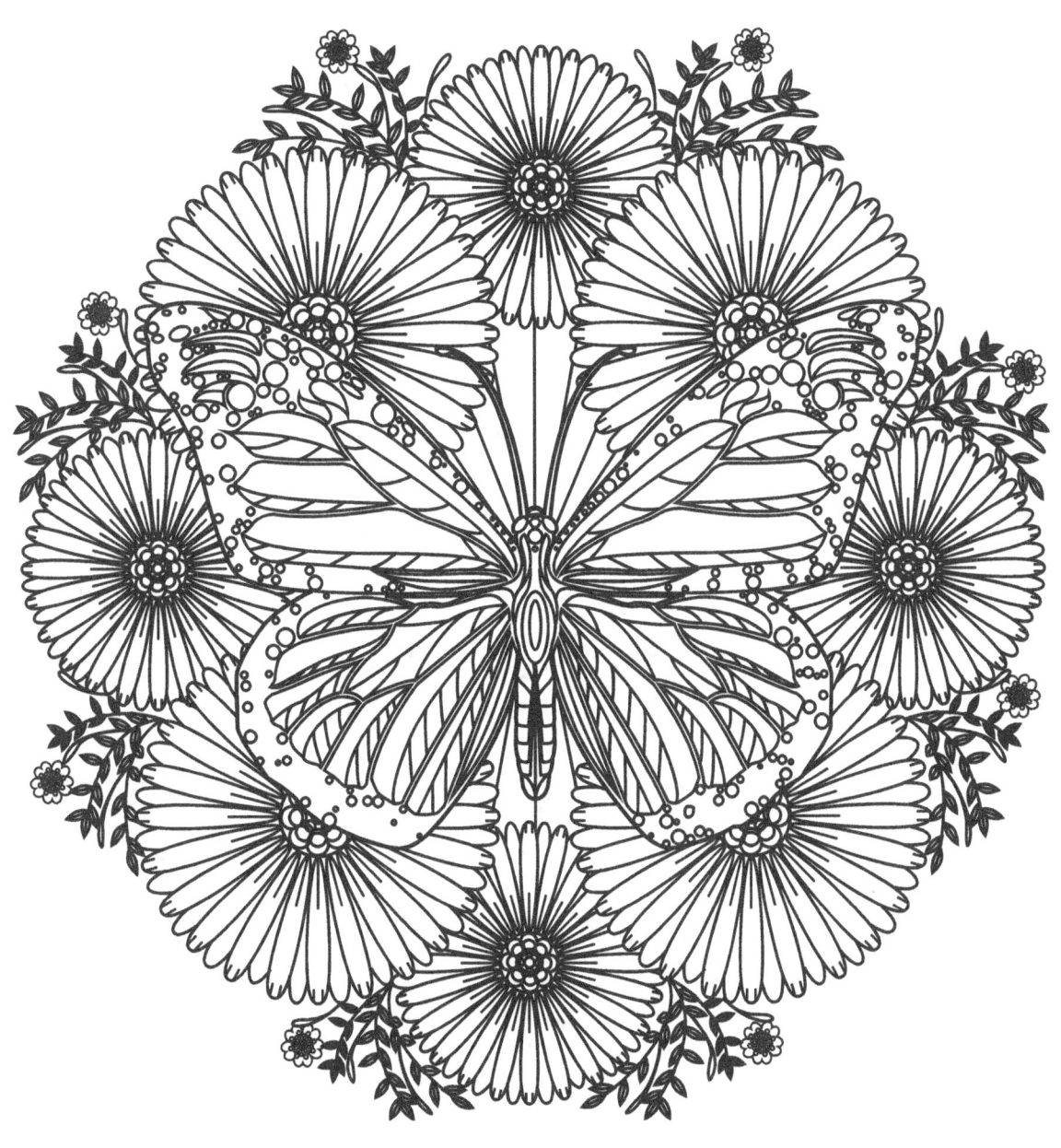

The Butterfly symbolizes fortuitousness. Renewal and immortality are embodied in the Butterfly.

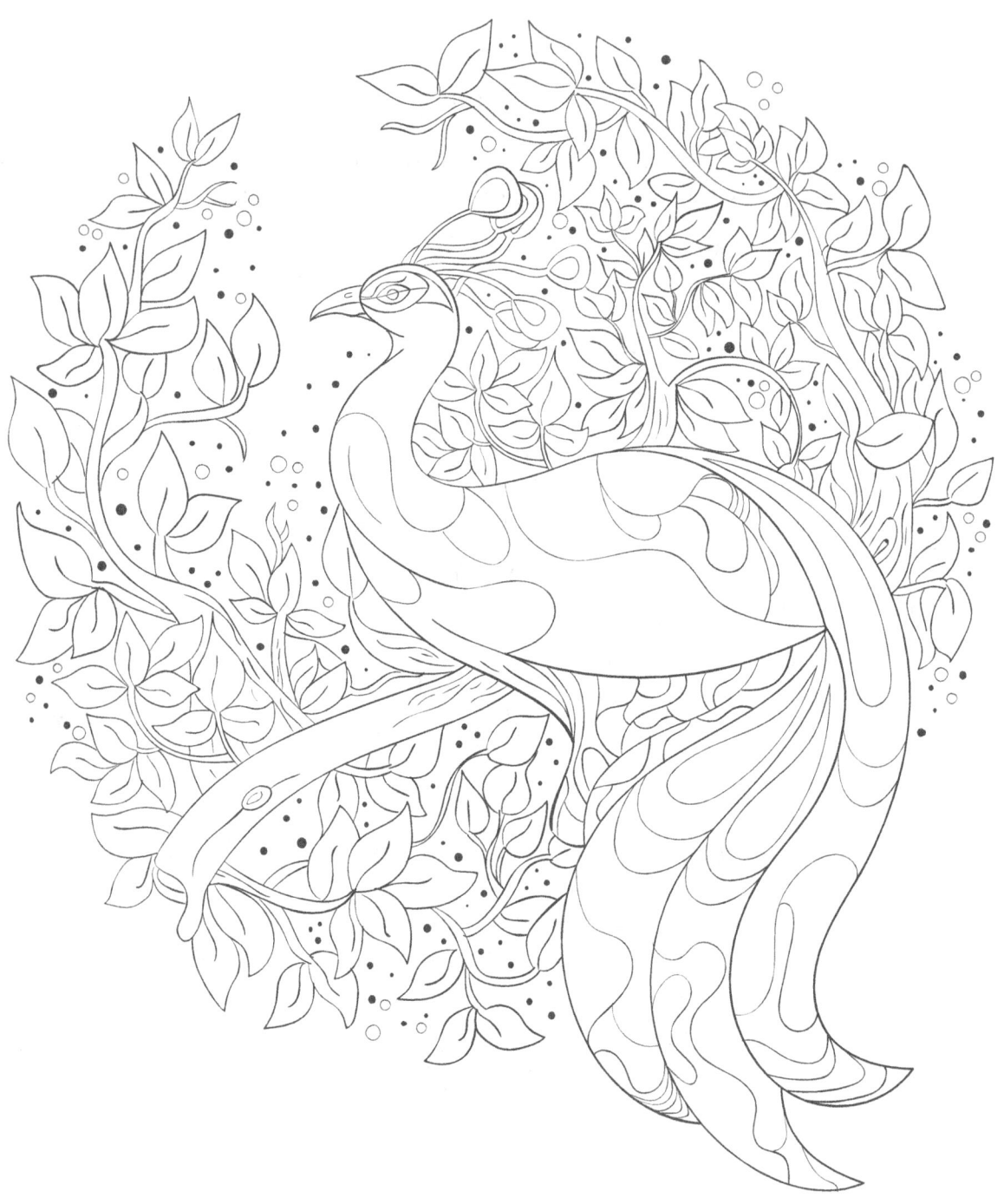

The Peacock is a symbol of good fortune. The peacock reminds
to stay balanced and honor ourselves.

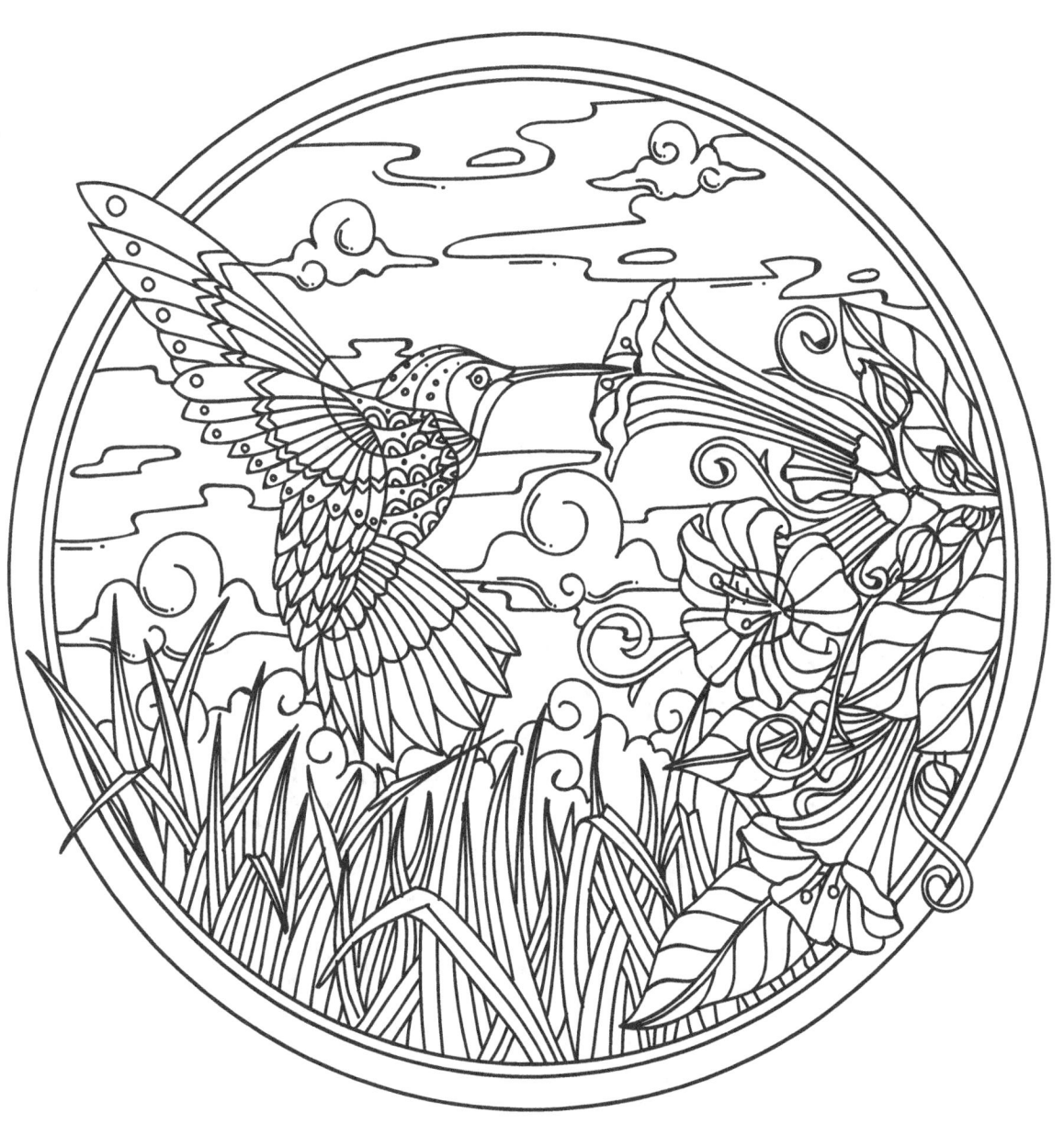

The Hummingbird is a symbol of brilliance and sophistication.
Emblemizing good luck and freedom.

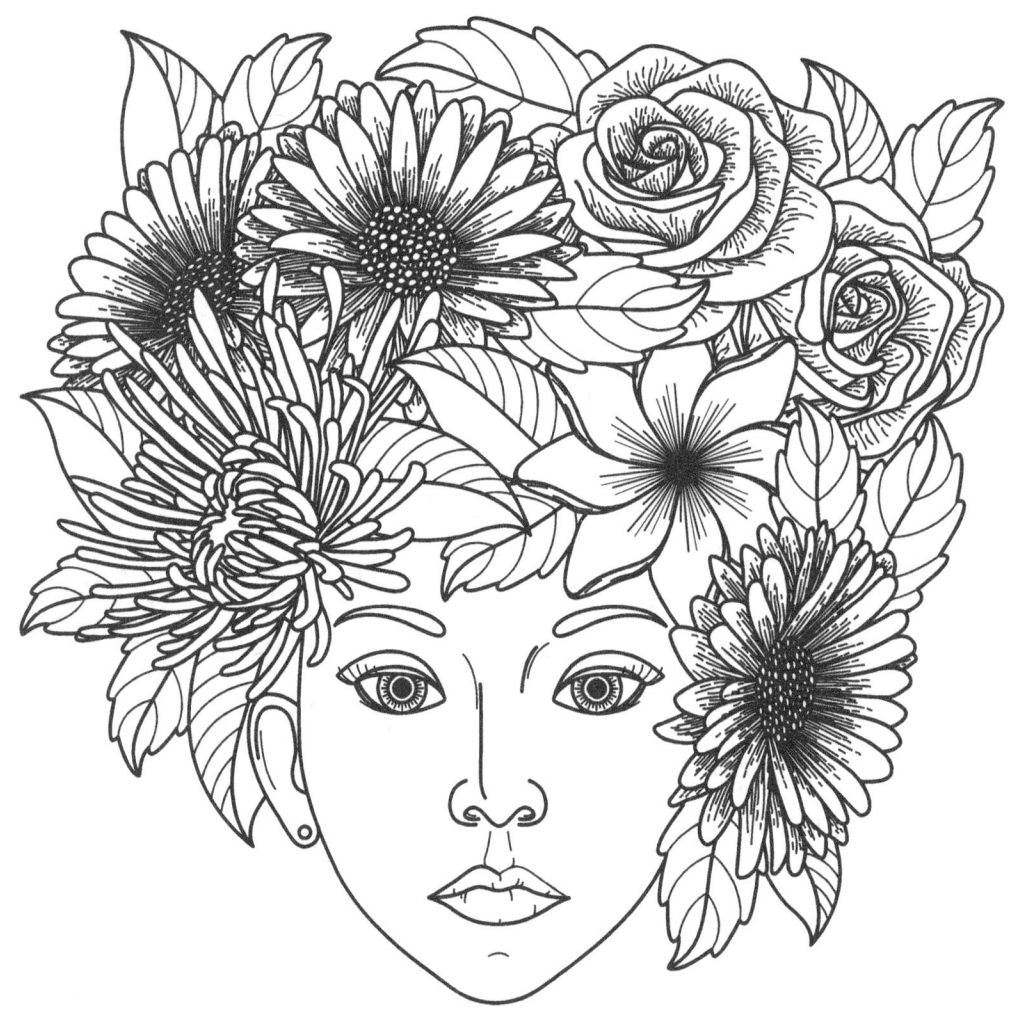

www.ingramcontent.com/pod-product-compliance
Lightning Source LLC
Chambersburg PA
CBHW082020230526
45466CB00022B/2894